# 8 MYTHS OF THE GREAT APOSTASY

# 8 MYTHS OF THE GREAT APOSTASY

## GREGOR McHARDY

SIGNATURE BOOKS | 2022 | SALT LAKE CITY

The opinions expressed in this book are not necessarily those of the publisher.

Cover design by Jason Francis.
Cover image is "Saint Peter," painted by Sir Peter Paul Rubens, c. 1616.

**FIRST EDITION** | **2022**

LIBRARY OF CONGRESS CONTROL NUMBER: 2022024747

Paperback ISBN: 978-1-56085-452-4
Ebook ISBN: 978-1-56085-427-2

# CONTENTS

# INTRODUCTION

Because of my current calling in my LDS ward, I get to sit in one of the comfy chairs on the stand. No, not the ones members of the bishopric sit in. Been there, done that, happy to move on. There is one drawback, though. In the days before COVID-19, everyone could see my face. Any reactions I made to what was being said or sung or played were immediately apparent to everyone. Oh sure, when it was just laughing at what the speaker said, no harm, no foul. But when some testimony went south or Brother Pompous was not watching the clock, I had to guard my reactions.

During one sacrament meeting address from a returned missionary, I am afraid I might have slipped. Her topic was the Restoration. In order to tell us why the Restoration was necessary, she recited the litany that has been chanted by many generations of missionaries: "After Jesus died and all the apostles were killed, the priesthood was taken from the Earth. After this, the church broke apart like a shattered mirror with everyone choosing to follow whatever little piece of the puzzle they wanted to. The truth was taken from the Earth, and for years and years there was no truth on the Earth. The whole world was in darkness. There was no light. [Yes, she actually said that.] Then came Joseph Smith." In case you are wondering, I committed at least seven grimaces and head shakes.

Granted, one of the grimaces was because of a mixed metaphor (shattered mirrors and puzzle pieces), but the other six were legitimate gripes about how she presented the great apostasy. If we are teaching the gospel truth, then we had better be darn sure that we are not basing it on a bunch of myths, misunderstandings, and outright lies. I think it is time we Latter-day Saints as a religious society stop blackening the memory of our own distant heritage in an attempt to make the shining wonder of Brother Joseph's vision more vivid.

I am on a quest pretty late in life to become a scholar. Heaven knows I failed miserably in high school; and for my undergraduate degree, I only did the work I needed to get passing grades. For the past several years, however, I have been pursuing a graduate degree in history, and this time it is not about the grades. I long had a passion for finding out exactly how the gospel of Jesus Christ became diluted and polluted; how his nascent church grew from local bishoprics to regional patriarchates to metropolitans and ultimately to popes. Years ago, I became dissatisfied with the curt explanations that I had given on my own LDS Church mission of how Christ's church had gone astray. I decided to read the millennia-old sources for myself and find out how it actually happened.

During my studies, like all professional students, I learned how little I know and how much more there is to learn. But I also learned a few details of which the average Latter-day Saint is probably unaware. I surmise this not only from statements such as those uttered by missionaries everywhere, but also by the disappointing experience I had reading a book by a fellow Saint on the topic. I had expected to get an inspired and scholarly account of what he called an inevitable event, but instead I found only superficial references to a few scholarly sources crushed under the immense weight of a doctrinal exegesis trying to prove that the great apostasy had been foretold. Oh, every word was gospel truth, but it was explaining history with scripture, and, as anyone who has tried to locate the Book of Mormon's city of Zarahemla has found out, such an endeavor can get a mite ticklish. I wanted to explain how the great apostasy actually came to pass from historical records.

Why the passion, you may ask. I believe understanding the apostasy historically is of great importance. Since childhood I have been fortunate to travel widely, and made one unforgettable visit to the Nazi death camps of Auschwitz-Birkenau. It is beyond the scope of this work to relate the horror of that visit, but one experience is germane. As we were told about the monstrous acts of soldiers herding people to their hideous deaths, I asked myself: how could relatively innocent young German soldiers have become monsters? I do not know (and, frankly, am not sure I care to know) the answer to that question, but its premise has become of great importance to me. What is the real difference between, for example, the Book of Mormon's first two opposites: Laman, a villain, and Nephi, a hero? In every LDS video ever produced, even the brand new ones, the evil brothers (Laman and Lemuel) are given the hirsute equivalent of a black hat. "Make no mistake, kids. These are the bad guys." But did they and Nephi not grow up in the same family, experience the same situations, and eat at the same dinner table? Are Laman and Noah and Korihor—other major characters in the Book of Mormon—simply two-dimensional bad eggs from whom we can learn nothing? Thanks to LDS writer Orson Scott Card, I have been able to see how relatively unimportant events and minor character flaws can end up with one brother tying up another brother to die a miserable death in the desert.

The same danger lurks in every one of our lives. If we are to survive the calamities that are said to descend upon us as the latter days grow ever later, any one of us may be torn from the bosom of truth. If there is already a wedge of falsity in our core beliefs, are we not in real danger, after letting go of the rod and tasting the real truth, of falling away into hidden paths? Could not each one of us, if we take the slightest small step away from truth, end up with a metaphorical black hat?

There are things we Saints believe about the great apostasy that simply are not true. Professing things that are not true in a setting where the Holy Spirit is supposed to testify of truth is counterproductive. Without the confirmation of truth, those learning our doctrine can be confused by or outright dismissive of what we present as the necessary conditions for the Restoration. Instead of presenting the clean-shaven face of truth, we are coming off with a five o'clock shadow.

## Do Not Skip This Part

There are several words or phrases that I use in this book that will make absolutely no sense to you unless you read the following.

First, let me introduce some acronyms I use. Latter-day Saints are comfortable calling the two parts of the Bible the Old Testament and the New Testament. We may, however, be unfamiliar with the fact that both these terms are mildly offensive to Jews. What comprises the first part of the Bible originally belonged to the Jews. Christians, originally being a Jewish sect, inherited it long ago, and renamed it *Old* in opposition to their *New*. But just imagine, if you will, that some group apostatized from our church, took The Book of Mormon with them, and rebranded it *The Lesser Truths* in opposition to their new book of scripture, *The Greater Truths*. We might be a bit perturbed. In this book then, let us use different terms, but which ones? While most scholars and theologians are very comfortable using the terms *The Hebrew Scriptures* and *The Christian Scriptures* to refer to the two parts of the Bible, Latter-day Saints are uncomfortable limiting Christian scriptures to the second half of the Bible, not to mention our perception of Christ in the first part. The Jews have a name for their part of the Bible: *Tanakh*, being an acronym for *Torah–Nevi'im–Ketuvim*, or "The Law, the Prophets, and the Sayings." Since the second part of the Bible was written in Greek, the corresponding acronym would be *Euepap* for *Evangélio–Epistolés–Apokálypsi*, or "The Gospels, the Epistles, and the Apocalypse." This is overly cumbersome, however. So instead of trying to make you retain Hebrew and Greek acronyms, I make use of English acronyms that have both clear meaning and cultural sensitivity: "The Law, the Prophets, and the Sayings" will become LP&S while "The Gospels, the Epistles, and the Apocalypse" will be shortened to GE&A. These fit in nicely with our own use of D&C, BoM, and PoGP for, respectively, Doctrine and Covenants, Book of Mormon, and Pearl of Great Price.

Second, how shall we refer to the Christian church after it began, as we Latter-day Saints believe, to apostatize? Latter-day Saints already have a term to refer to the church under Christ and the apostles: the primitive church. However, this book addresses a time after the primitive church, but still before the establishment of the Christian church in the fourth century CE. The most common term historians use is the "proto-orthodox church," which points toward the organization that was comprised of the "right faith." But since Latter-day Saints see this process not as moving toward the right faith, but away from it, this term becomes problematic. So instead of referring to the church in transition by where it was heading, I refer to it by comparing from whence it came: the "post-primitive church."

Third, a word about the dating system used in this book. Many Latter-day Saints are of the opinion that if one uses CE (Common

Era) instead of AD (Anno Domini, or year of our Lord), one may be agnostic. Yet there are many faithful Christians who opt for CE. I am one of them. The base year for the AD system was not designated until about eight centuries after Christ's birth by a certain Dionysius Exiguus, and he was off by several years. When you actually do the math correctly, you find that Jesus was born from three to seven years before tradition says he was. So instead of fumbling around with a faulty system, I opt for the much-easier-to-designate Common Era (CE) with its corresponding Before Common Era (BCE). Also, if one happens not to be Christian, it stands less of a chance of provoking offense.

## Why This Book Is Different

The great part about the introduction of a book is that you can usually skip it and still get the information you came for. For that reason, I am going to hide this section in the introduction. It is called a historiography, or the history of what historians have said on the topic.

Historiography was my least favorite and lowest graded class in my degree program, but it needs to be here so that anyone who might pick up this book can tell that I have tried hard to do the necessary homework on the subject matter.

In researching this book, I browsed through the extensive book catalogs of LDS publishing houses trying to find anything that would shed light on Mormon perspectives of the great apostasy. The results were dismal. Barely half a dozen works have been published on the matter over the last century.

The most recent book on the great apostasy was written by Tad R. Callister, *The Inevitable Apostasy and the Promised Restoration* (2006). It is written not by a scholar, but by an LDS general authority (he was released in 2014). As such, Callister's aim was not so much to explain how the events actually went down, but how they were *prophesied* to have gone down, and what they mean in a teleological framework. I misunderstood this when I purchased and read his book several years ago. I had hoped to get a story of how things actually happened, but instead was presented with a scriptural exegesis of how it had been foretold and what that means to the modern Latter-day Saint. This is not a critique of Callister; he did his job well. It is just a disclaimer that an analysis of his work does not have place here, as his book is primarily exegetical.

James E. Talmage's *The Great Apostasy* (1909), while being heavy on scriptural exegesis, claims to be a historical analysis of the reasons behind the event. (Talmage's book was published before he was ordained an LDS apostle in late 1911.) He says that "the evidence of the decline and final extinction of the primitive church among men is found in the scriptural record *and in secular history.*"[1] He further states, "In our study of the predictions of the apostasy as embodied in scripture and of their realization as attested by later history, we will recognize two distinct phases or stages of the progressive falling away as follows: 1) apostasy *from* the church; and 2) the apostasy *of* the church.[2] Clearly Talmage intended this book as an historical study as well as a doctrinal work.

Talmage is legendary among Latter-day Saints due to the 1915 publication of his *Jesus the Christ*. Talmage's study is one of the few books on the approved reading list for active missionaries, and a fair portion of LDS Church membership has been instructed and inspired by this influential book. When one hears that Talmage also wrote *The Great Apostasy*, the cachet of his name automatically influences one to give it the same credence. I do not believe that the same divine guidance that informed his later work was present in the former. In the following critique of Apostasy, I mean no disrespect to the man, but only the weakness of his method in this early instance.

Talmage had a good education, although his training was in the sciences and not history. Before his elevation to the apostleship, he was an influential educator in Utah. While the language used in the book is elevated and articulate, the supporting scholarship is somewhat lacking. When scholars propose to write, the first thing they do is pull together as much of what has been written about the subject as they can possibly find, both books that support his thesis and also those that offer contradictory viewpoints. It appears Talmage relied on but a few books favorable to his views. Just for comparison's sake, the 50,000-word thesis that I wrote for my MA degree contained just over 500 citations from 178 sources. One quarter of

---

1. Talmage, *Great Apostasy*, I; emphasis mine.
2. Talmage, *Apostasy*, 32.

those sources were "primary sources," which are immediate, first-hand accounts of a topic from people who had a direct connection with it. Secondary sources are accounts that interpret or analyze the primary sources. By comparison, *The Great Apostasy*'s 75,000 words are backed up by 243 citations from thirty-two sources. Fully 48 percent of Talmage's citations were from the scriptures, with another 26 percent from only three secondary sources: Gibbon, Milner, and Mosheim (see below). Only three primary sources are used, totaling less than 3 percent of the citations.

Talmage's book was meant to be both doctrinal and historical, but basing the majority of the historical side on only three authors, all of whom are secondary sources, is somewhat less than a thorough investigation.

Not only is Talmage's work based on a very few sources, but their quality can also be questioned. Gibbon is the famous author of the unparalleled *The Decline and Fall of the Roman Empire*, published in 1776. While it is still read today, and was extensively read in Talmage's day, modern professors shy away from encouraging students to use it as a source for historical scholarship because it is a bit long in the tooth. I believe that one can still find gems in Gibbon's work, including his groundbreaking pronouncement that the stories about early Christian martyrdom were extremely exaggerated. Between Gibbon's credibility and Talmage's closer proximity to its publication, we can have a fair amount of trust in what Talmage quotes from him. However, the same does not apply to Joseph Milner's *History of the Church of Christ* or Johann Lorenz von Mosheim's *An Ecclesiastical History*.

Talmage's book makes use of footnotes almost exclusively for scripture references. In other instances he directs the reader to "See Note 1," which is at the end of the chapter. Here he quotes entire paragraphs or pages from either Mosheim or Milner. Talmage quotes Johann Mosheim's *Ecclesiastical History* some thirty times. Mosheim was a German scholar who wrote in Latin. His work was subsequently translated into English by a British doctor of divinity named James Murdock in 1868. Christian scholars at that time were a bit put off by Gibbon's somewhat agnostic approach to the Christian religion in his *Decline and Fall*, hence both Mosheim's original and Murdock's English translation consists of bombastic rhetoric that demeans paganism and elevates Christianity with little regard to a fair and balanced report of either. Here, Mosheim defines the native religions of Europe:

> So that, however different the degrees of enormity might be, with which this absurd and impious theology appeared in different countries; yet there was no nation whose sacred rites and whose religious worship did not discover a manifest abuse of reason and very striking marks of extravagance and folly.[3]

True, it was a different time, and it would be anachronistic to confront Mosheim with the practices of political correctness. But complete vituperation of a way of life and worship that Mosheim neither understands nor documents is not scholarship, but merely diatribe. While writing about ancient mystery cults—religions whose rites were kept absolutely secret for centuries—he says,

> The secret of these institutions was kept in the strictest manner, as the initiated could not reveal anything that passed in them without exposing their lives to the most imminent danger; and that is the reason why, at this time, we are so little acquainted with the true nature of the real design of those hidden rites. It is, however, well known that, in some of those *mysteries*, many things were transacted that were contrary both to real modesty and outward decency.[4]

First, he says, "we are so little acquainted," but in the next sentence he says, "it is well known." It is either one or the other, not both. Also, while Mosheim documents the former part of the statement, his second supposition is completely without support. The incident to which he is opaquely referring is the Bacchanalia scandal of 186 BCE in Rome. The scandal focused on an ostensibly religious organization, originally just for women, that met occasionally to perform rites of worship focused on Dionysius. Over time, however, since part of the worship included giving one's self over to the altered state of drunkenness, the rites began to degenerate. Men were allowed to participate, which led to debauchery; other crimes, such as perjury,

---

3. Mosheim, *Institutes of Ecclesiastical History*, 22.
4. Mosheim, *Institutes*, 27–28.

forgery, and alteration of wills, were also committed.[5] The Roman state severely punished the criminals convicted in the scandal and sharply limited the group's further activities. This one isolated incident hardly merits the broad brush with which Mosheim indicts mystery cults generally. Other mystery cults, such as the Eleusinian mysteries, which endured for a thousand years, may more readily be compared with LDS temple rites than with pagan bacchanalias.

The other work heavily favored by Talmage was Joseph Milner's *The History of the Church of Christ*, a massive, five-volume work published between 1794–1809. In a way, Milner is simply writing Mosheim in English. And, following the prevailing tradition of his time, he sounds like a pompous Cambridge theologian looking down his nose at anything that does not support the full glory of everything Christian.

In the end, whether due to lack of other sources in his library or simply his liking of Milner and Mosheim, Talmage based almost his entire book on ultra-conservative sources that read history in one direction. But those voices were so congenial to his outlook, and his voice so persuasive to our willing ear, that we rely on the weight of Talmage's name to inform our earliest traditions of the Great Apostasy.

Another LDS work focusing on the great apostasy, *Outlines of Ecclesiastical History*, was published forty years later by the eminent B. H. Roberts. He was a brilliant man, a servant of the Lord, and a prolific writer. But he was not a trained historian.

Roberts's book was written as a textbook, so it presented facts meant to be consumed and memorized, complete with quizzes at the end of each chapter. It is obvious that Roberts relied heavily on Talmage, as his notes include the same historians: Gibbon, Mosheim, Canon Farrar, and the Oxford Bible Dictionary with a sprinkling of Eusebius.

Roberts's section on the great apostasy starts out with an account of how all Jewry deplored Christians and united to try to wipe them off the face of the Earth. He supports this by describing the martyrdoms of Stephen, James of Zebedee, and James of Alphaeus as if any Jew of the time would have happily participated. He cites

---

5. Robinson, *Criminal Law of Ancient Rome*, 38.

Mosheim accusing the Jews of inciting the Romans against Christians. Because of the weight of the "traditions of the fathers" that he had unwittingly inherited, Roberts perpetuates the medieval anti-Semitic tradition we have all inherited that Jewry, "an imperious nation," is collectively responsible for the death of the Savior.[6] At the outset of his book he says that "the enfeebled world was tottering on its foundations," despite the fact that the Western world at that time was experiencing the greatest peace it had known for centuries, something that Roberts acknowledges a few pages later. He states that all religions at the meridian of time were "negative creeds," "destitute alike of spirit and of life."[7] In doing so, he appears to have injected an anachronism (creeds were a Christian invention two centuries from inception), but also forgets that Greek and Roman religions were an integral part of the moral and social fabric of those highly civilized societies. He labels Roman religious worship as "absurd and ridiculous; and what is worse yet, debasing, obscene and cruel." A good historian would provide examples of such things to establish this argument as fact. Roberts asks us only to rely on his authority.[8]

We get insight into Roberts's approach when he analyzes the supposed Roman persecutions of Christians. He says that Rome leaned toward religious freedom and wonders why the Romans would single out the "mild and beautiful Christian religion." But instead of following this thread to any historical conclusion, he concludes that it was the nebulous and nefarious powers of Satan.[9]

Roberts's greatest weakness is shown when he refutes the idea that Peter was designated as the leader of the primitive church. His rejection of the "Rock of Revelation" concept (which I discuss as Myth 2), while not new, certainly shows how deeply it was embedded in the Mormon psyche at this time. His argument (which I will not cite here) is based on the rules of English grammar, disregarding the fact that Jesus spoke in Aramaic. This is similar to the argument of what the doctrine is depending on where one places the comma in

---

6. Roberts, *Outlines of Ecclesiastical History*, 116–17.
7. Roberts, *Outlines*, 20.
8. Roberts, *Outlines*, 22.
9. Roberts, *Outlines*, 119.

"Verily I say unto you today thou wilt be with me in paradise," when commas are a later, European invention.

Roberts's *Outlines* does not introduce much new material to the discussion of the great apostasy, but simply echoes and encourages Talmage's opinions.

Perhaps a critical reading of Roberts's textbook is what spurred the creation of T. Edgar Lyon's *Apostasy to Restoration*. Lyon was a teacher employed by the LDS Church's Seminary and Institute program. His study was also published as a textbook, but for the Melchizedek Priesthood quorums of the LDS Church Sunday School program in 1960 (much like the *Teachings of the Presidents of the Church* series from 1997 to 2016). And some of it was actually ... good! Too bad it was published in a church manual, where no one would ever read it. However, this manual would astonish any twenty-first-century Saint, so habituated are we to the constraints of our highly correlated church materials. The first chapters include discussions about the Eleusinian mysteries, the cult of Bacchus, and the nature of Roman religion. Were I to mention such items in my elders quorum class, more than a few eyebrows would be raised and some self-appointed guardian of doctrinal purity would scuttle towards the bishop's office. Would not the ward bishop be surprised to find that I had been quoting from a book whose copyright holder is none other than David O. McKay?

Lyon starts his work stating that he is not trying to find the point at which the apostasy happened, but simply trying to describe what took place within Christianity.[10] He also gives a cogent summary of the two main doctrinal points upon which the apostasy hinges: the understanding of the nature of the Godhead and of Christ.[11] He makes a decent case that faulty Christologies, especially Docetism, were the first impurities to creep into pure doctrine. This work takes time to acquaint readers with the events and personalities that formed the early church, telling the stories of Polycarp, Justin Martyr, Irenaeus, and Tertullian. Further chapters discuss Martin Luther, Ulrich Zwingli, John Calvin, and the German and English Reformations. Here is a work that can teach the novice the whole history of the time between Simon Peter and Brother Joseph Smith—not just scriptural

10. Lyon, *Apostasy to Restoration*, 4.
11. Lyon, *Apostasy*, 6–7.

exegesis. One of the best points Lyon makes is distinguishing between Christianity being "illegal" and "outlaw." Christians were not illegal by their very existence: you could not go out and round up a bunch of Christians and execute them. They were simply outside the protection of the law when it came to other exigencies.[12]

Although Lyon was a scholar and a thoughtful man, he too was a product of his time and limited by concurrent historical research. He states unequivocally that by 100 CE apostolic leadership had vanished and that plans to perpetuate any general church leadership were entirely absent—points that I refute in chapters two and three.[13] He holds to the canonical ten persecutions of Christians by the Roman Empire—something that has been debunked by recent research.[14] His prejudice against non-LDS beliefs glares from his condemnation of post first-century "Christians" as unacceptable to Christ in any form—a statement that seems to stand in stark opposition to the premise of his book.[15]

Coming shortly on the heels of Lyon's work was an essay from the indomitable BYU religion professor Hugh Nibley called "The Passing of the Church: Forty Variations on an Unpopular Theme," originally published in *Church History* in 1961. Nibley's strength lies in his having seemingly read everything under the sun in every language, but this also leads to his greatest weakness: a rambling narrative that bounces off various sources like a pinball—a result of all that genius leaking all over the page at once. Another BYU religion professor, Kent P. Jackson (see below), says that Nibley generalized excessively, saw things in sources that simply do not seem to be there, and let his predetermined conclusions set the agenda for the evidence.[16] I have not managed to read much more than a few pages of Nibley at once. Frankly, it exhausts me. Perhaps my lack of understanding of Nibley shows more of my own weakness as an historian, and my critique of his work points more toward me than him. But in reading "Passing," I knuckled down and tried to follow

---

12. Lyon, *Apostasy*, 22.
13. Lyon, *Apostasy*, 3.
14. Lyon, *Apostasy*, 22.
15. Lyon, *Apostasy*, 4.
16. Jackson, "Leaving the Facts and the Faith," 107–22.

things through, only to come to the same conclusion as Jackson, even before I read Jackson's critique.

For example, Nibley states "Jesus announced in no uncertain terms that his message would be rejected by all men," for which he has seventeen citations from the GE&A.[17] It takes a long time to look up all those references (including the time to decipher his Roman numerals), and when one is done, one wonders whether that is what Jesus really said. He attributes "the most tragic disorganization and confusion follow[ing] hard upon the passing of the apostles" to Hegesippus' declaration that after the apostles had passed, error began first to creep into the church—a clear example of seeing something that was not there.[18] He also states that when Jesus said that the gospel would go to the ends of the world and then would come the end, the end Jesus had in mind was the great apostasy, even though a few verses later the Son of Man is to appear in heaven.[19] This is clearly an example of "predetermined conclusions [setting] the agenda for the evidence." On several occasions Nibley tries to prove a negative—for example, arguing that there was no Sunday school for Christian kids and that there was no concerted missionary effort on the part of the apostles, just a vindictive testimony to condemn those that would not listen anyway.[20] The fact that we do not have any primitive-church Primary song books is not proof that they did not exist. Nor does the absence of any of the apostles' speeches after 49 CE prove that all they did was testify and leave. However, Noel B. Reynolds (see below) states that it was Nibley's work that launched LDS scholarship into a phase of interpreting the great apostasy through scholarship of newly discovered texts. Nibley indeed opened the Saints' eyes to many new sources, but he used them to justify the prevailing thesis propounded by Talmage and Roberts: that the apostles made no provision for the future and that even Christ had not meant for his church to endure past the death of the apostles.

Whatever the impact of Lyon's insightful textbook and Nibley's exhausting essay, the Saints wandered in the wilderness of Talmage

---

17. Nibley, *The Passing of the Church*, 2.
18. Nibley, *Passing*, 7.
19. Nibley, *Passing*, 2; Matt. 24:14, 30.
20. Nibley, *Passing*, 6–7.

for almost the full proverbial forty years until Kent P. Jackson published *From Apostasy to Restoration* in 1996.

In 1987 I had the privilege of touring Western Europe with the
BYU Singers, singing our way from Belgium to Budapest. Acting
as an official representative for the university was Dr. Jackson and
his wife, Nancy. I have nothing but fond memories of this delightful couple with their endless patience and good nature. When my
search through books about the apostasy turned up his name, I was
even more delighted. Jackson's book, unfortunately, only has twenty
pages that intersect with the subject matter of this book. Although
Jackson properly references copious quotations from the GE&A, he
also quotes extensively from other primary sources (multiple works
by at least eleven different authors) and secondary sources including
Bo Reicke, Stephen Robinson, Dallin Oaks, and Robert Millett.

Jackson begins by saying that the word chosen by Paul to describe
the "falling away" is *apostasía*, which comes from *hístemi*, meaning "to
stand," and *apo,* meaning away from. Jackson says the word describes
not a fall from grace, but an active rebellion. He also claims that
this apostasy was already a weedy garden a mere two decades after
Christ had been resurrected, and fully gone to seed by 100 CE.[21] He
correctly identifies John as having already castigated Docetism in
the first century (2 John 1:7), but his supposition that 1 John 4:2–3
identifies the same problem should perhaps be reconsidered, as a
comparison to D&C 129 would make Joseph Smith a Docetist.[22] In
condemning Gnosticism, Jackson has followed many other scholars
who believe Irenaeus' description of the sect is accurate, when it is
probably as accurate as much anti-Mormon literature is in our own
day.[23] While Jackson, who is an expert on ancient scripture, is comfortable interpreting Revelation as pertaining to particular historical
events or geographical locations, my experience has shown that using anything from that baffling book in a historical work is folly.[24]

In the third chapter, Jackson notes that with the passing of John
around 100 CE, "the keys of the kingdom were *taken*," and that there

---

21. Jackson, *From Apostasy to Restoration,* 9, 13.

22. Jackson, *Apostasy,* 15.

23. Jackson, *Apostasy,* 14.

24. Jackson, *Apostasy,* 16.

is no more evidence or indication of the calling of other apostles.[25] He goes so far as to posit that Jesus instructed his apostles to *stop* perpetuating the Twelve.[26] There is absolutely no proof of, or precedent for, the second statement, and I provide evidence in chapter three that the first statement is also not correct.

Jackson does do a good job of showing examples of where apostasy was creeping into the post-primitive church, especially with the example of Ignatius' farewell tour and Polycarp's adulation.[27] However, in his recitation of example after example of Paul, John, Peter, or Jude reproving the false doctrines or bad behaviors creeping into the membership of the church, he fails to recognize that behind every misbehaving believer or wayward leader were a multitude of faithful saints who were doing their absolute best to follow the gospel. When they received these admonitions, it likely caused the people to grow in faith and righteousness. Remember that in the Book of Mormon there are 529 pages that recount the problems, and only two that speak of the blessedness of the primitive Nephite church. We tend to dwell on the negative in order to thwart it, but that does not mean goodness ceases to exist.

Interestingly, Jackson chooses Clement of Rome's *Epistle to the Corinthians* to make his point. He admonishes those saints for trying to replace their apostolically appointed leaders with others more to their liking. This is indeed indicative of error creeping into the church. But as I point out in Myth 3, the very passage quoted by Jackson reinforces the fact that the apostles had set up a way to replace church leaders and sustain those in office.[28] History may be read pessimistically or optimistically. I believe that, on the whole, Jackson has leaned to the side of pessimism in order to create a tidy box into which to put a quick and dirty rebellion. Putting things in tidy little boxes is what historians often do. I am guilty of it myself. I think that we need to acknowledge that history is a lot more quick and dirty than we like.

Published just a year before Callister's *Inevitable Apostasy* was a

---

25. Jackson, *Apostasy*, 19. Italics mine.
26. Jackson, *Apostasy*, 22.
27. Jackson, *Apostasy*, 25–26.
28. Jackson, *Apostasy*, 24.

compilation of scholarly articles regarding the Christian apostasy, edited by Noel B. Reynolds, called *Early Christians in Disarray* (1995). (Dr. Dursteler's contribution to the Reynolds volumes, "Inheriting the Great Apostasy," acquainted me with most of the volumes I have discussed above.) Reynolds notes that in the 1960s Richard L. Bushman, later of *Joseph Smith: Rough Stone Rolling* fame, noted that just as one cannot reconstruct the shattered mirrors and windows of an accident scene into a reliable account of a car accident, historians needed to stop focusing on how the ordinances mutated or the doctrine morphed, as this does not reveal the *causes* of the apostasy.[29] In order to understand the apostasy correctly, Reynolds writes, one must engage in some myth busting. Here is his own list of myths: (1) the apostasy happened because of persecution; (2) it was instigated by the Hellenization of Christianity; and (3) like my Myth 8, the Roman Church is the great and abominable church.

Several articles in the book, including Richard E. Bennet and Amber J. Seidel's "A World in Darkness," John W. Welch's "Modern Revelation," and James E. Faulconer's "Concept of Apostasy," while well written and informative, do not intersect with the content of this book. John Gee's "Corruption of Scripture," Daniel W. Graham and James L. Siebach's "Introduction of Philosophy," David L. Paulsen's "Divine Embodiment," and Noel B. Reynolds's "Decline of Covenant," while meriting further research for a more complete story of what the great apostasy *was*, are beyond the scope of this work, which is about what the great apostasy *was not*.

Readers have probably realized by now that my intended audience is Latter-day Saints. However, I have tried to provide enough context so that readers unfamiliar with LDS teachings, terminology, etc., may still find the material interesting and thought-provoking.

In concluding this brief introduction, let me give a short acknowledgement to Kent (Kip) Larsen, the man largely responsible for the inclusion of these last several pages of historiography. I got to know Kip during my senior year of high school when his father presided over the LDS Silver Spring Stake and for a couple of months while I dated his sister. After forty years of occasionally coming across his name in

---

29. Reynolds, *Early Christians in Disarray*, 3.

LDS publishing circles, I decided to look him up and ask for advice on getting this book published. He was gracious enough to remember our short acquaintance and friendly enough to gently take me to task for some holes that I still had in my manuscript and methodology.

Now, on to the book.

# TWELVE APOSTLES WERE ALL MARTYRED

It is commonly thought among Christians of all denominations, including the Church of Jesus Christ of Latter-day Saints, that, except for John, all of Jesus' original twelve apostles were killed. A 2005 *Ensign* article conceded that "we do not have records of the deaths of all the apostles," but still made the assumption that "the apostles were killed."[1]

In another *Ensign* article, the author states without any reservation that "no tradition about the early church is more firmly held than that 'all the apostles except John were martyrs.'"[2] Why is this belief so prevalent?

We Latter-day Saints should be better informed. We claim to have in the Book of Mormon another testament of Jesus Christ. And in that other testament, there are twelve men selected to preside over the affairs of the church. They are called disciples instead of apostles, but their function is identical. How many of them died to seal their testimony? As I recall, nine of them wrapped up their affairs on their seventy-second birthday and blissfully crossed the rainbow bridge (3 Ne. 28:3). The other three, like John, never did die. Why do we believe that one set of apostles had to die in order to fulfill their God-appointed office, but that their equivalents in Zarahemla got off more easily?

It is not because of any modern revelation, but rather the result of a widely held belief we inherited from the Christian tradition. Members of the post-primitive church were enthralled with martyrdom. There was a definite subset of these saints who believed

---

1. Shanna Butler, "What Happened to Christ's Church?" *Ensign*, Feb. 2005.

2. Andrew C. Skinner, "Apostasy, Restoration, and Lessons in Faith," *Ensign*, Dec. 1995.

that if a Christian died an unjust and agonizing death, he was on the fast track to heaven because he had emulated Jesus' death.[3] We Latter-day Saints are no different. If we hear of a missionary dying in the field or a patron passing in the temple, we are likely to say that we "can't think of a better time to go," meaning, "That guy's going straight to heaven." We believe that the smear of a testator's blood is a glowing, celestial cherry on top of a lily-white life, no matter that it is the Savior's blood that changes our crimson rags to snowy robes.

William W. Phelps's hymn of beatification to Brother Joseph, "Praise to the Man," is cross-referenced to D&C 135 where John Taylor states that "The testators are now dead, and their testament is in force." This in turn is linked to Hebrews 9:16, where the KJV says, "For where a testament is, there must also of necessity be the death of the testator," which has led many to think that a belief for which one is killed is of more force and efficacy than one for which one dies of old age in bed. A more informed translation of this passage, however, simply states: "For where there is a will, the death of the one who made it must be proven," which means that a death certificate is necessary before anybody's last will and testament can be executed. Paul was just telling us that Christ's new covenant could not be in force until after his death; it has no reverse connotation that a saint needs to die a martyr's death in order to establish a true witness. Yes, Joseph and Hyrum were murdered, and, yes, their blood cried from the Earth against their murderers. But to think that martyrdom was requisite for them to establish the church, just as Christ established his covenant, is a little over the top. In this chapter we take a look at what we actually know of the original twelve apostles and how they died.

But perhaps we ought to get to know them first. Quick, close your eyes and name as many of the Twelve as you can. There's Peter, James, and John, doubting Thomas, and Judas Iscariot … and, oh, yeah, Matthew. If you got more than these six, you are better than most. But before you get down on yourself, remember that the scriptures do not really give us an entirely clear picture of who the Twelve were.

---

3. Perkins, *Suffering Self*, 18.

There are four places in scripture where the original Twelve are listed: Matthew 10, Mark 3, Luke 6, and Acts 1. The lists in Matthew and Mark agree with each other, but since Matthew largely copied Mark's account, this is not surprising. Since Luke wrote both Luke and Acts, those lists are the same as well. There is a discrepancy between the two sets, however—more than just the fact that Luke calls Simon by his nickname, Peter. Take a look at the problematic numbers ten and eleven below.

| | Matthew & Mark | Luke & Acts |
|---|---|---|
| 1 | Simon | Peter |
| 2 | James, son of Zebedee | James, son of Zebedee |
| 3 | John, son of Zebedee | John, son of Zebedee |
| 4 | Andrew | Andrew |
| 5 | Philip | Philip |
| 6 | Bartholomew | Bartholomew |
| 7 | Thomas | Thomas |
| 8 | Matthew (Levi) | Matthew (Levi) |
| 9 | James of Alphæus | James of Alphæus |
| 10 | Simon the Canaanite | Simon Zelotes |
| 11 | Lebbæus Thaddeus | Judas (James's brother) |
| 12 | Judas Iscariot | Judas Iscariot |

Now that we know the names of the apostles, we can begin to consider what records we have about their lives and deaths outside of the scriptures. And we can also discuss the discrepancies in this list.

The original twelve apostles of the LDS Church were called in February 1835, but it was not until over two years later that Heber C. Kimball, Orson Hyde, and five others spearheaded the church's first effort to "preach the gospel unto all the world." Likewise, the original Twelve of the primitive church fulfilled various ministering opportunities during the decade or so after Christ's resurrection. But apparently that all changed at the culmination of the Council of Jerusalem in about 49–50 CE—the abbreviated conference report of which is recorded in Acts 15. While this biblical record does record the calling and sending of Paul and Barnabas, it does not mention any of the other apostles receiving calls or being sent out. Other sources, however, tell us that there was a meeting of the Twelve where the lands of the world were divvied up—whether by casting lots or by assignment is unclear, but each apostle received his own territory.[4] Certainly each apostle had a staff of persons, probably including a member or two from the seventy, roughly analogous to today's area presidencies. But the apostles did not just end up willy-nilly going here and there preaching to the ends of the Earth. But be prepared for a little more "ends of the Earth" than you may have thought previously. In the following pages we discuss the lands, both far and near, they ended up going to, and where they most likely died, consulting an author named Hippolytus, a second-century church leader.

We are also going to talk about their remains, or relics. If the apostle John had saved his nail clippings, he could have sold them for their weight in diamonds to some medieval king. Both noble and common folk during medieval times thought that the remains of a holy person still carried the essence of holiness about them, and that being in close proximity to such remains could bring them healing or forgiveness. Many of us are not so different. Just look at the long lines of Latter-day Saints who eagerly wait to greet an apostle visiting their stake conference. But back in medieval Europe, if your local church could boast the head of Andrew (purportedly in Amalfi, Italy) or a finger bone of John the Baptist (of which so many exist that the man must have had several hands), you could put up a souvenir shop in front of your church and rake in the shillings from pilgrims. A discussion of the stories of apostles and their demise necessarily mentions where his body purportedly lies today.

## 1. Simon Peter

"Peter preached the Gospel in Pontus, and Galatia, and Cappadocia, and Betania, and Italy, and Asia, and was afterwards crucified by Nero in Rome with his head downward, as he had himself desired to suffer in that manner."[5]

---

4. Rhodes, "Acts of Andrew and Matthias," 453; Eusebius, *Church History*, 2.25.8.
5. Hippolytus, *On the Twelve Apostles*, 254–55.

"Antioch, and Syria, and Cilicia, and Galatia, even to Pontus, received the apostles' ordination to the priesthood from Simon Cephas, who himself laid the foundation of the church there, and was priest and ministered there up to the time when he went up from thence to Rome on account of Simon the sorcerer, who was deluding the people of Rome with his sorceries. The city of Rome, and all Italy, and Spain, and Britain, and Gaul, together with all the rest of the countries round about them, received the apostles' ordination to the priesthood from Simon Cephas, who went up from Antioch; and he was ruler and guide there, in the church which he had built there, and in the places round about it."[6]

The GE&A do not explicitly say that Peter ever went to Rome. Peter writes from a metaphorical "Babylon" in his first epistle, and the history of the Gospel of Mark (which is actually the Gospel According to Peter, only written by Mark) places Peter squarely in Rome.[7] There are, however, many extra-scriptural traditions saying he both lived and died there. We investigate much more about his career in a separate chapter. For now we can say that there are documented traditions that put Peter's death at about 68 CE in Rome, probably under the hand of the Emperor Nero and most likely in the middle of the stadium that Nero had built in what is now called the Vatican.[8] The reason for Peter's arrest had to do with public disputes he had with one Simon Magus, that disreputable character converted by Philip in Samaria who had previously been a magician, and who coveted the apostle's ability to bestow the Holy Ghost (Acts 8:5–13). The stories of their disputes include such things as levitation, reanimated dried sardines, talking dogs, and soliloquizing babies—so the details can be disregarded.[9] Peter's ultimate victory over Magus brought him great notoriety, but ultimately led to his demise.

Four women—Agrippina, Nicaria, Euphemia, and Doris—were concubines of Agrippa, a high Roman official. They converted to the Christian gospel and decided they would no longer engage with Agrippa. These women, apparently not understanding that it was not

---

6. Anonymous, *Teaching of the Apostles*, 671.
7. Hengel, *Saint Peter*, 103.
8. Eusebius, *Church History*, 2.25.8.
9. Rhodes, "Acts of Andrew," 313–17.

the sex itself that was sinful, but the illegitimate nature of it, convinced Xanthippe, the wife of one of Nero's close friends, Albinus, to abandon her own perfectly sanctioned marriage bed. Eventually the two men found out about their shared problem and made plans to have the women followed to Peter's church meetings. Xanthippe heard of the plot and warned Peter. Although Peter considered it cowardly, his brethren convinced him that if he ran away, he could at least continue preaching. And so he quickly disguised himself and fled from Rome.[10]

Classic movie buffs may recall the 1951 film *Quo Vadis,* featuring such names as Deborah Kerr, Peter Ustinov, and an uncredited Elizabeth Taylor. The movie's title comes from a dubious tale that just as Peter was exiting the city gate, he saw Jesus shaking his head and walking into the city. "Where are you going [*quo vadis* in Latin]?" the stunned Peter asked. "To Rome to be crucified," was the terse reply. "You're going to be crucified *again*?" Suddenly it dawned on Peter that the vision meant that since Peter was neglecting the duty of dying for his people, the Lord would have to do it himself. He sheepishly took off his disguise, re-entered the city, and gave himself up to the authorities.

Tradition has it that Agrippa had Peter crucified as a way of mocking his religion, but that Peter, deeming himself unworthy to emulate his Lord that way, asked to be crucified upside down.[11] Many Christians believe that this is what was meant by Jesus' prophecy "when thou shalt be old, thou shalt stretch forth thy hands" in John 21—his hands would be stretched out on the cross. But immediately afterward, Jesus tells Peter "another shall gird thee, and carry thee whither thou wouldest not," which does not seem to bear the interpretation out.

Unlike any other apostles, with the possible exception of Paul, we know the exact plot of ground upon which Peter was killed. The emperor Caligula had begun building a great stadium for chariot races in what was then the countryside outside Rome. The oblong island in the middle of the track around which the chariots raced was filled with monuments, at the center of which was an obelisk that had

---

10. Rhodes, "Acts of Andrew," 332–33.
11. Jerome, *Lives of Illustrious Men,* 361.

been imported from Egypt. It was next to this obelisk that people were executed as a part of game-day activities. If Nero executed Peter, this is where it would have happened. We know exactly where that obelisk stood, for among all the obelisks in Rome, this is the only one that was never toppled. It was moved from its original spot to the center of St. Peter's Square when the current St. Peter's Basilica was constructed in the sixteenth century, but its original base was marked by a stone that is still to be found in a quiet courtyard in Vatican City that is called the *Piazza dei Protomartiri Romani*, or Plaza of the First Roman Martyrs.

Romans, along with almost every other ancient society, did not allow burials within the city limits, so cemeteries were either crowded up against city walls or located somewhere in the suburbs. But in contrast to the kinds of cemeteries Americans are familiar with, Romans built whole houses, complete with sculptures, paintings, and many receptacles for the bodies, bones, or ashes of family members. These houses were all built together in what is known as a necropolis, or city of the dead. One such necropolis was on the hillside just outside the northern walls of Caligula's stadium.

Since this necropolis was so close to the stadium, it was convenient to dump the bodies of executed persons here, about 300 feet from where they had been killed. Certainly, on the day that Peter was killed, one or two church members must have witnessed the execution and followed the undertaker to the hole into which Peter's body was deposited. In the days following his death, his followers probably visited his grave on a regular basis, because that is what you did if you were an ancient Roman. And one of those saints placed some ceramic tiles to mark the spot where Peter was buried. Then, sometime around 200 CE, a man named Gaius had a memorial built over the ceramic tiles. It consisted of a pair of columns holding up the front half of a shoulder-high shelf whose back half was anchored in the wall of a stairway going up the necropolis hill. On top of the shelf was a pair of pilasters (decorative, non-weight-bearing ornaments that look like pillars, found in many LDS temple ordinance rooms today) that led up to a pediment (a squat, elongated triangle like the one on the front of Greek and Roman temples). The shelf was probably meant as a respectful receptacle for memorial offerings with which Romans festooned their sepulchers, like the balloons, candles, flowers, and stuffed animals placed at modern intersections where a beloved person tragically died. In a time when things were built for the ages, this memorial was sure to have been standing proudly when Constantine the Great had the original St. Peter's Basilica constructed with its high altar placed right over Peter's grave.

As part of this fourth-century building project, the ground for the new basilica needed to be leveled (it was a hillside in those days). The result was that the Roman necropolis was itself buried. Twelve hundred years later when this original basilica was demolished to make way for the new St. Peter's Basilica, the architects added another sixteen feet of fill over the old elevation in order to support the massive piers that would support the massive dome atop that massive building. However, the central portion of the building was not covered, leaving the descending curving staircases down which Ewan McGregor descends in Ron Howard's film adaptation of Dan Brown's *Angels and Demons*. There is still a holy of holies called the *Confessio* at the base of those stairs. I vividly remember standing by those steps as an elementary schoolboy, being told that this was where Peter was buried. This already jaded Mormon, who had seen too many of John the Baptist's fingers, thought to himself, "Uh huh, and the Ark of the Covenant is under that altar." But, as it turns out, under that holy of holies lies something truly startling.

In the thick of World War II an archaeological project excavated under St. Peter's Basilica in order to find and verify Peter's supposed grave. The extensive necropolis was discovered and later opened to visitors. A few years ago, my wife and I traveled to Italy to meet our daughter after she completed her LDS proselytizing mission. As part of the post-mission tour, we stopped in Rome and spent a day in the Vatican. Our first stop was a guided tour of the necropolis. After a dozen or so such sepulchers, I was greeted with an astounding sight, even though I knew it was coming. There, behind protective glass, with ancient dirt still clinging to it, was the left pillar of Gaius' memorial still holding up a corner of the shelf. Surrounding us was graffiti left by saints 2,000 years ago. After winding through a few more passages under the *Confessio*, we came to the other side of Gaius' memorial where a retaining wall had been built in antiquity to mark off Peter's grave. In an ancient niche carved into this wall was a Greek inscription saying, "Here is Peter." A small bag of bones mixed with dirt had been placed inside as well. The Catholic church has issued a statement that the bones in that niche are from a first century, sixty-something-year-old male, and have proclaimed them to belong to Peter. A few pieces of those bones have been encased in Lucite and are reverently displayed. Indeed, the tour guide ceased from her prattle at this point and allowed us three or four minutes of silence "to worship."

I am not able to tell you whether these are indeed Peter's bones. This much I can tell you, however. The next time I stood symbolically as Peter in an LDS temple, my perspective was completely different. Having more closely regarded his service and death, and having been close to the place where so many of his followers had venerated his legacy for so many years, I had a deeper respect and understanding of him. Perhaps this is what is experienced by the thousands of our friends from other denominations who venerate the remains of the apostles and other saints.

## 2. James, Son of Zebedee

"James, his brother, when preaching in Judea, was cut off with the sword by Herod the tetrarch, and was buried there."[12]

"Jerusalem received the ordination to the priesthood, as did all the country of Palestine, and the parts occupied by the Samaritans, and the parts occupied by the Philistines, and the country of the Arabians, and of Phœnicia, and the people of Cæsarea, from James, who was ruler and guide in the church of the apostles which was built in Zion."[13]

James is known today as James the Greater to distinguish him from the other James lower on the list. He is John's brother. Since he is always mentioned first of the pair, we assume he was the older of the two and that he would have been what Latter-day Saints would call the first counselor in the first First Presidency of Peter, James, and John. Besides Judas Iscariot's death, James's death,

---

12. Hippolytus, *On the Twelve Apostles*, 255.
13. Anonymous, *Teaching of the Apostles*, 671.

at the order of Herod Agrippa, is the only apostolic death recorded in the GE&A. This Herod was the grandson of Herod the Great, who rebuilt the Jewish temple and presided over the events in Luke 2. Herod Agrippa reigned as subject king under the Roman Empire from 41–44 CE. It was at this time that the mad emperor Caligula tried twice to get a statue of himself erected in the Jewish temple, but Herod Agrippa persuaded him to desist, for which the Jews were very grateful. Even though Herod Agrippa was not a Jew, Jerusalem pretty much adopted him. It is perhaps as part of Herod's zeal toward his adoptive people that he took action against the zealous proselytizing of the primitive Christian church—and James was a vocal proponent of that church, so much so that the GE&A calls him "a son of thunder."[14] Luke tells us that Herod Agrippa had both Peter and James jailed, and then executed James with the sword (Acts 12:2). The supposition is that James was beheaded, but since Herod was trying to ingratiate himself to the Jews, and the Jews did not allow beheading, James was probably run through with the sword.[15] Herod Agrippa got such a positive response from the Jews at Jerusalem that he put Peter next on the docket.

Since around 1150 CE, the location of James's execution has been said to be on the site of the Armenian Cathedral of St. James at the base of Mount Zion in Jerusalem. In case you are interested, the Armenian Apostolic Church never had any ties to the Roman Church but claims apostolic succession directly through Bartholomew. The Armenian Church is subdivided into two geographic regions, the main one being, of course, in Armenia; but it also has an official presence in Jerusalem, complete with a patriarch. St. James is this patriarch's cathedral, or the official place of his seat (from the Greek κάθωμαι, kathomai, or seat). Church officials claim that James's head is retained in a rich chapel on the left side of the cathedral, where Jesus' mother Mary supposedly buried the head.[16] Since James was probably not beheaded, this is doubtful. Whatever the cathedral actually has, it only

---

14. MacDonald, *Does the New Testament Imitate Homer?*, 137.

15. Polhill, *Acts*, 278.

16. Armenian Patriarchate of Jerusalem, St. James Cathedral, www.armenian-patriarchate.com/st-james-cathedral. Though this was my source, the address is no longer functional.

claims James's head, leaving all kinds of room for the growth of one of the most imaginative relic traditions in Christian tradition.

If you have been to or read much about Spain, you might be familiar with the fact that St. James is its patron saint, bearing the nickname St. James the Moor Slayer. What's that, you say? James killed Muslims? In Spain? Eight centuries after he was martyred? According to a twelfth-century tradition, when King Ramiro I's Christian army was in danger of being overrun by an unnamed Muslim emir at the Battle of Clavijo in north-central Spain in 834 CE, James appeared on a white horse and rallied the beleaguered Christian troops to an impossible victory. The Battle of Clavijo is completely fictional (not to mention James's apparition) but the whole account has been believed and promoted over the last millennium, continuing to rake in millions of pilgrimage Euros annually, even today.

Spain was known to the early Christians. Indeed, some think that Paul visited there late in his life. But there is no record of early Spanish Christian communities. However, in the twelfth century CE a tradition began to grow in the northwest corner of the peninsula that, like Paul, James had visited that corner of Spain. The story goes that after his death in Jerusalem, his body was miraculously placed in a boat that was piloted by angels from the Judean coast, through the Straits of Gibraltar, and around the Portuguese coast to the northwestern tip of Spain. The legends get mixed up at this point. Either the divine ship foundered and the body washed ashore intact, or a knight fell from a cliff into the sea, or a bride's horse was spooked and ran madly into the surf, but whether it was the corpse, the knight, or the damsel in distress, something came out of the surf covered in scallop shells. No mention of how the body came to be buried. Some eight centuries later a monk wandering through the neighborhood claimed to see a "field full of stars" that led him to the grave of the saint: hence *campostella* (field of stars). A cathedral was built over the site, Santiago de Campostella, which became so famous that pilgrims from all over the European continent walked from as far away as Germany, 500 miles away, to visit it. If they completed the pilgrimage, they received a scallop shell. Untold millions have trodden the trails leading to Santiago de Campostella over the millennium. The trails have become the

European version of the Appalachian Trail, with over 300,000 pilgrims joining in the hike in 2017 alone.[17]

An interesting side fact is that James seems to be the only apostle recognized by the LDS Church as being a saint. If you attend a temple session in a Latin language, you will hear the second apostolic messenger call himself some version of Santiago. How does one get Santiago from James? Well, the *iago* part is the Latinized version of James. Shakespeare uses it in *Othello*. The *Sant* part is obviously the same word as our *saint*. In Catholic tradition, all the apostles are called saints, but whereas St. Peter is a little tricky to pronounce, *Santiago* rolls right off the tongue. So if you live south of the border and your name is James, your friends may think they are just saying Jimmy, but they are really saying Saint James. Think of that the next time you listen to the LDS temple endowment ceremony in Spanish or Portuguese.

### 3. John, Son of Zebedee

"John, again, in Asia, was banished by Domitian the king to the isle of Patmos, in which also he wrote his Gospel and saw the apocalyptic vision; and in Trajan's time he fell asleep at Ephesus, where his remains were sought for, but could not be found."[18]

"Ephesus, and Thessalonica, and all Asia, and all the country of the Corinthians, and of all Achaia and the parts round about it, received the apostles' ordination to the priesthood from John the evangelist, who had leaned upon the bosom of our Lord; who himself built a church there, and ministered in his office of Guide which he held there."[19]

When we say that all the apostles were killed, we must admit that we know of at least one who not only was not killed, but did not even die: John the Beloved. LDS scripture proclaims that he was, like the Three Nephites in the Book of Mormon, translated to some sort of immortality. Christian tradition admits that John at least was not

---

17. Editorial Buen Camino, "Estadística de Peregrinos del Camino de Santiago," *Camino de Santiago*, accessed Sep. 6, 2021, editorialbuencamino.com/estadistica-peregrinos-del-camino-de-santiago.

18. Hippolytus, *On the Twelve Apostles*, 255.

19. Anonymous, *The Teaching of the Apostles*, 671.

killed, but probably lived in the ancient city of Ephesus (currently Selçuk, Turkey) until around 100 CE. A church was built over a grave in which he was supposedly buried.

According to the *Acts of John* from the late second century, when his time came, John constrained two men to take baskets (buckets) and shovels and to go dig a very deep trench. When it was done, he took off everything except his underclothes, laid them in the bottom of the trench, offered up a very long prayer, and then lay down on his clothes at the bottom of the trench. After one final "Peace be with you, brethren," he promptly expired. However, one source says that an extremely bright light hovered over his grave for an hour. The assembled brethren apparently only covered him with a linen cloth and went home, proposing to come back and bury him the next day. When they returned, however, the body was gone. All that remained were his sandals. They concluded, after remembering what the Lord had said to Peter, that he must have been translated.[20] Hippolytus records that sometime in the reign of Trajan (98–117 CE) John "fell asleep at Ephesus, where his remains were sought for, but could not be found."[21]

With that in mind, consider a name you might encounter when reading non-LDS material on John: "St. John the Divine." People who use this term are not making some sort of judgment about his godly status. John's title is meant to bestow *theological* preeminence on him. His gospel, which is the only one that gives a clear picture of Jesus' nature and calling, warrants his classification as a theologian.[22]

You need to know that there has always been a great controversy among Christian scholars about the authors of the Gospel of John, the author of the three Epistles of John, and the author of the Book of Revelation, and whether they were all one and the same John. This disagreement is not confined to modern scholarship; even early Christian scholars (like Eusebius, who wrote in 325 CE) were concerned that perhaps the writer of Revelation was not John the apostle. Latter-day Saints, however, have the prophecy of Nephi that indeed identifies the author of Revelation as the apostle.

---

20. Rhodes, "Acts of Andrew," 268–70.
21. Hippolytus, *On the Twelve Apostles*, 255.
22. Shelton, *Quest for the Historical Apostles*, 131.

Speaking of the Book of Revelation, John records in its first chapter that he was writing it on the island of Patmos after being exiled there. There are many theories put forth about what landed him there, including Tertullian saying that in Rome "the apostle John was first plunged, unhurt, into boiling oil, and thence remitted to his island-exile."[23] It was Hippolytus who provided the name of the emperor who sent him off: Domitian (81–96 CE).[24] The spot where this supposedly happened is marked by a little church with the most delightful name: *St. John in Oleo*. The current structure was built in the sixteenth century, but it was constructed over the foundations of a much earlier church dating back as far as the fifth century. There is, however, no record of John even being in Rome, much less being boiled. The reason for him being on Patmos remains a mystery.

After being released from Patmos, John is known to have lived around the city of Ephesus where he would have come into contact with and ordained Bishop Polycarp, who is discussed below.

What is not known from documentation, but can easily be deduced from a little reasoning, was stated very poignantly by W. Brian Shelton: that there eventually came a time in Christian history when there was but one living apostle remaining—only one man alive that had walked and talked with Jesus.[25] Whatever the location and circumstances of John's last days were, he would certainly have a right to wallow in a bit of nostalgia before shuffling off whatever it was he left in that trench.

Before going any further with the apostles, we should point out what one of the landmark scholars of antiquity has said about the subject. Edward Gibbon, who authored the massive *Decline and Fall of the Roman Empire*, wrote that by about 240 CE the recorded martyrdoms of the apostles were limited to Peter, James (Son of Zebedee), and Paul. The martyrdoms of all other apostles were added at later times.[26] In other words, we need to take each of the following stories of martyrdom with a heaping dose of skepticism.

---

23. Tertullian, *Prescription Against Heretics*, 260.
24. Hippolytus, *On the Twelve Apostles*, 255.
25. Shelton, *Quest*, 125.
26. Gibbon, *History of the Decline and Fall of the Roman Empire*, vol. 2, 20.

## 4. Andrew, the Brother of Peter

"Andrew preached to the Scythians and Thracians, and was crucified, suspended on an olive tree, at Patræ, a town of Achaia; and there too he was buried."[27]

"Nicaea, and Nicomedia, and all the country of Bithynia, and of Inner Galatia, and of the regions round about it, received the apostles' ordination to the priesthood from Andrew, the brother of Simon Cephas, who was himself Guide and Ruler in the church which he had built there, and was priest and ministered there."[28]

In a fanciful *Acts of Andrew* (probably composed around 250 CE), Andrew goes about in Greece and other territories as far away as the modern-day Ukraine working mighty miracles. Greece and Ukraine are worlds apart. Even with modern transportation it took me a half day of flying and two days of driving to get from Athens to Ukraine. But an ancient document that correctly lists the mission calls of Peter, James, John, and Thomas also lists Andrew as having served in these regions, so it is not beyond belief.[29] Today a beautiful baroque church stands on the site of an eleventh-century church, supposedly marking the spot where Andrew climbed a hill, placed a cross, and prophesied that a great city would someday stand there.

The *Acts of Andrew*, however, includes a long recitation of completely unbelievable miracles. Gregory of Tours, who abridged the document in the sixth century, left out a ton of stuff that "bred weariness," for, as Shelton agrees, "it is not the multitude of words, but the soundness of reason and the purity of mind that produce unblemished faith."[30] The miracles included calling down an earthquake on an incestuous mother just as Andrew and her falsely accused son were about to be sewn into leather bags and cast into the sea. He apparently converted the wife of the Roman administrator of Patras, a port city on the west coast of Greece. But the administrator was vexed about the unsettling of his life and condemned Andrew to be crucified. Like Peter, however, Andrew counted himself unworthy to suffer death in the same manner as Jesus.

---

27. Hippolytus, *On the Twelve Apostles*, 255.
28. Anonymous, *Teaching of the Apostles*, 671.
29. Anonymous, *Teaching of the Apostles*, 671.
30. Rhodes, "Acts of Andrew," 337.

When Andrew was led out to his execution, he addressed an ode to his instrument of death and then willingly submitted, having his hands merely tied (not nailed) to the cross so that he would die from starvation and exposure, not bodily trauma. Over the next several days he held forth about the worthiness and timeliness of his coming death. The townsfolk of Patras were so alarmed by a criminal spouting such virtuous proverbs that they called on the administrator to pardon him. The administrator was just about to take him down when Andrew, seeing his glorious martyrdom about to slip away, quickly soliloquized and gave up the ghost. The *Acts of Andrew* sounds as if it was written by Parson Weems, George Washington's first biographer, who embroidered Washington's life with such apocryphal tales as that of the cherry tree and the silver dollar. Perhaps Andrew did travel to the Greek colonies along the shores of the Adriatic and Black seas. Perhaps he even died at Patras. But the fact that such a glorious death is not attested to until after 250 CE gives us reason to doubt it. The crucifixion one-upmanship over his brother Simon Peter makes it even more suspect.

Today you can find Andrew's relics, or the report of them, all the way from Istanbul to Scotland. While he was reportedly buried in Patras, Greece, a significant portion of his relics were transferred to Constantinople, perhaps when Constantine was gathering monuments and memorabilia from all over the Roman Empire to adorn his newly built capitol around 325 CE. However, when the Western European crusaders pillaged Eastern Europe's Christian capitol in 1204 CE, they made off with all sorts of precious commodities, taking them back to Amalfi, Italy. There they are still, mostly tucked away from sight under the main altar, but sometimes exuding a dense substance that the locals call manna which is collected and revered.

Andrew's skull is another matter. Mary Sharp records that in 1462 Pope Pius II had Andrew's head transferred to Rome, where it stayed until 1964.[31] In a gesture of goodwill between Roman Catholic and Greek Orthodox churches, Pope Paul VI decided to return the skull to the Cathedral of St. Andrew in Patras, nicely presented in a gold reliquary shaped like Andrew's face. McBirnie reports that sometime

---

31. Sharp, *Traveller's Guide to the Churches of Rome*, 15.

after it arrived, a pious vandal who could not abide religious statuary in the round (Greek Orthodox prefer two-dimensional portraits or icons), removed the bones and smashed the gold reliquary. The relics were then placed in a less offensive silver reliquary.[32] The only problem is that, while one can view a skull in Patras, one can also view a golden reliquary in Amalfi that purports to be the back of Andrew's skull. Perhaps this piecemeal approach to relic distribution is how we end up with so many remains of so many saints throughout the world.

Another tradition says that before the bulk of the relics were carted off to Constantinople, a monk from northern Britannia named Regulus received a divine calling to hide the relics in the farthest corner of the world. Regulus pilfered a tooth, an arm bone, a kneecap, and some fingers and headed back to what is now Scotland. There they were kept and venerated, thus making Andrew the patron saint of Scotland. Some of the remains were destroyed by Scottish Presbyterians during the Reformation. In 1969 Pope Paul VI ordained Joseph Gray as the first Scottish cardinal in four centuries and gifted him one of the remaining relics. They can now be seen at the National Shrine of Saint Andrew, St. Mary's Roman Catholic Cathedral in Edinburgh.

The Scots call their national flag the Saltire, as Americans call theirs the Star-Spangled Banner. According to legend, a Scottish king named Angus prayed for divine help in his battle against Athelstan back in 832 CE, fifteen miles east of Edinburgh. Some kind of cloud formation was then observed that looked something like an X, or St. Andrew's cross. Centuries later the legend culminated in the current flag. You can see that same white cross on the Union Flag of Great Britain, formed by welding together the St. George's Cross (England), St. Andrew's Cross (Scotland), and St. Patrick's Cross (Northern Ireland). So, yes, you've probably come across the St. Andrew's cross many times without having known it; but now you know.

## 5. Philip

"Philip preached in Phrygia, and was crucified in Hierapolis with his head downward in the time of Domitian, and was buried there."[33]

---

32. McBirnie, *The Search for the Twelve Apostles*, 83–84.
33. Hippolytus, *On the Twelve Apostles*, 255.

Because Philip shared his name with one of the seventy, early Christian scholars had a hard time keeping them straight. Poor Eusebius got them hopelessly mixed up, so we are not sure whether anything he said about Philip was about the apostle or the seventy. Local legend in the city of Pamukkale in west central Turkey (called Hierapolis in Philip's time) says that he died around 80 CE, which would make him rather old. A report dating from a century later comes from the bishop of Ephesus (about 150 miles from Pamukkale) stating that Philip was buried in Hierapolis along with his two elderly virgin daughters. (Another joined them soon afterward.) No mention of violent death. Another source says that Philip of the seventy had four virgin daughters, so this account seems to have more to do with the seventy than the apostle.

*The Acts of Philip*, dating from the fourth century CE, provides a much more colorful story of Philip's death. In this story, Philip preaches in Hierapolis along with his sister, Mariamme, and Bartholomew. They preach with enough success that the city's governor sentences them to death. Bartholomew is nailed to one wall and Philip is hung by hooks through his heel bones from the opposing wall. There, they smile at each other because they are about to die in the Lord's name. John the Beloved shows up and tries to dissuade Philip from cursing the city. But he is unsuccessful and Philip's curse causes a sinkhole to open up in the middle of the city and drag down the potentate along with about 7,000 townspeople. This is too much for Jesus, who appears and asks why Philip is so unmerciful. Jesus draws a magic cross in the air whose foot descends into the sinkhole, allowing the 7,000 to crawl out. But he leaves the official in the abyss. Jesus tells Philip that he will eventually be able to come to paradise, but that he must first endure forty days of buffeting outside the gates of heaven. Philip directs the townsfolk to unpin Bartholomew and release Mariamme (who will go on to die elsewhere). But when they come to take Philip down off his hooks, he berates them, soliloquizes about eternal life, and voluntarily dies.

In W. Brian Shelton's recent and masterful analysis of the various and jumbled stories of the apostles, he proposes criteria for evaluating the veracity of each one. One criterion is, "the more extreme the miracle ... the more the credibility of the source diminishes." He also posits that relics with long lines of tradition and very little competition may be regarded as more authentic.[34] By these criteria, the arguments for Peter's and Paul's tombs and traditions are greatly bolstered, as they are very ancient and completely singular. Philip's seems less authentic because of the outlandish miracles, but Patras seems a feasible resting place, and thus a good beginning for his trail of relics.

The grave of this person, whoever he was, had a church built over it in the sixth century. At some point, some of his relics were transported to Constantinople. From there a foot and some teeth made their way to the Church of the Holy Apostles in Rome, where the relics were venerated as belonging to Philip and James of Alphæus.

## 6. Bartholomew

"Bartholomew, again, preached to the Indians, to whom he also gave the Gospel according to Matthew, and was crucified with his head downward, and was buried in Allanum, a town of the great Armenia."[35]

It is worth noting that although all four lists of apostles mention Bartholomew, his name is never mentioned anywhere else in scripture. That may be because he had another name. Someone named Nathanael is mentioned a couple of times in association with the apostles in the GE&A, specifically during John's discourse about how the apostles were chosen and during the post-resurrection scene at the Sea of Galilee. Many scholars, including those who wrote the LDS Bible Dictionary, think that Bartholomew and Nathanael are actually the same person. After all, "Bar" simply means "son of," so maybe he is Nathan MacTholomew.

If you visit medieval cathedrals in Europe, you may come across a rather grotesque depiction of a man with no skin. This is Bartholomew, who was supposedly skinned alive. A larger-than-life, anatomically correct bronze statue of San Bartolomeo stands in the cathedral in Milano, Italy, sporting realistic musculature from head to toe, and carrying his skin draped over his shoulders. A slightly less horrific version was painted by Michelangelo on the altar wall of the Sistine Chapel. The resurrected Bartholomew sports regenerated

---

34. Shelton, *Quest*, 45, 56.
35. Hippolytus, *On the Twelve Apostles*, 255.

skin but dangles a ghastly skin suit that purportedly looks a lot like Michelangelo himself. Whether his skin is present or not, Bartholomew is always depicted with the knife that flayed him.

Legend has it that Bartholomew traveled to Armenia where he converted the king, whose brother took umbrage at the act and had him skinned—or was it crucified—or both? The name of the king is nowhere to be found in the annals of Armenia, but there is a king of that same name and time frame in India. Indeed, traditions have Bartholomew appearing in Iran, Iraq, Egypt, Turkey, and the shores of the Black Sea.

As for his relics, the earliest arrived in a town currently on the border between Turkey and Syria in the early sixth century. But somehow his bones later washed up on the shore of Sicily where they were interred in a lead coffin, around which was built a church bearing his name. Someone who thought that this little place was not important enough for such relics carted them off to Benevento (fifty miles northeast of Naples). Then, about 150 years later, they were again trundled off to more auspicious quarters on a little island in the Tiber River in Rome. The Frankfurter Dom in Germany claims to have Bartholomew's skull, while Canterbury, England, claims a hand.

## 7. Thomas

"And Thomas preached to the Parthians, Medes, Persians, Hyrcanians, Bactrians, and Margians, and was thrust through in the four members of his body with a pine spear at Calamene, the city of India, and was buried there."[36]

"India, and all the countries belonging to it and round about it, even to the farthest sea, received the apostles' ordination to the priesthood from Judas Thomas, who was guide and ruler in the church which he had built there, in which he also ministered there."[37]

One often reads faith-promoting stories on the internet that are long on details but short on names, dates, and locations. A quick trip to Snopes or TruthOrFiction quickly puts such stories to rest. As we have seen in several of the foregoing accounts, modern fact-checking refutes

---

36. Hippolytus, *On the Twelve Apostles*, 255.
37. Anonymous, *The Teaching of the Apostles*, 671.

some of the claims about the apostles. However, in the case of Thomas, too many names and dates are mentioned for the story to have been completely fabricated, although there is certainly some embroidery. We have to say that the story of Thomas is "based on actual events."

Several years after Jesus' resurrection, some records say as late as 54 CE, Thomas made his way to the Indian subcontinent. *The Acts of Thomas*, a much later work that spells out his travels and miracles, states that, like Jonah, he was unwilling to go to India and had to be divinely convinced. However, and whenever, he set out, there were certainly Jewish colonies along the west coast of modern India that could at least understand his language. He apparently had much success there, creating churches in as many as seven or eight different cities. There is a Christian sect in the area whose members still have long genealogies going back to the first or second century CE. Indeed, a writer named Ibn Daisan (Arabic) or Bardesan (Aramaic) wrote sometime prior to his death in 222 CE that there were Christians in India who claimed to be descended from Thomas's converts. His account does not include any mention of Thomas's death. A century or so later, however, the prolific author Ephrem the Syrian reports on a merchant arriving in Edessa (in modern-day Turkey) on an errand from King Mazdai bearing many of the relics of Thomas, who had been speared to death by a previous Indian king. Curiously, a king named Bazdeo (a different pronunciation of Mazdai) appears on Indian coinage from the period, and linguists admit that the two names are cognomens. Marco Polo includes in his famous book that he encountered Christians in India in the thirteenth century who said Thomas had been their apostle. So we safely presume that Thomas did indeed minister to people in India. The story of his death cannot be entirely discounted either, especially since it is not wrapped in fantastic legends.

What can be disputed are the subsequent legends that have cropped up about him. Like Marco Polo, Thomas is reputed to have gone all the way to China and then to Indonesia. These travels are only hinted at, however, and have no supporting names, places, or dates.

There is even a report of him having preached in Paraguay. It is impossible, of course, but there may be a buried kernel of related truth. According to an Austrian missionary named Martin

Dobrizhoffer who worked in Paraguay in the 1700s, a local chieftain told him that they did not need the gospel because it had already been preached to them by "Father Thomé." Martin heard the name *Thomé* and immediately associated it with the doubting apostle. But since the chieftain was unfamiliar with the LP&S and GE&A and was simply quoting a name, might not that name be a cognomen for Timmy, the diminutive form of Timothy? I mean, after all, wasn't Timothy, the brother of Nephi who was raised from the dead, one of the candidates for the Three Nephites? This is, of course, wild conjecture, but interesting.

Remember that merchant who brought some of Thomas's relics to Turkey? King Mazdai did not send *all* of Thomas's bones with that merchant. He retained a reliquary in Chennai where some of Thomas's remains were venerated until the place was completely razed by invaders. The remains that did make it to Syria were transferred sometime prior to 1258 to a Greek island called Chios—with the possible exceptions of a shard of femur, which is now displayed in the ancient monastery of Mar Mattai in northern Iraq, and Thomas's head, which is reputed to be held on the island of Patmos. In 1258 a pirate named Ortona Leone had a spiritual experience in a Chios church. The local priest, probably hoping to save the gold and silver plate, attributed the pirate's experience to some bones he claimed were relics of Thomas. Leone copped a leg bone and loved it so much that he came back the next day, gathered up the whole hoard, and shipped it back to Ortona, Italy. The collection is now housed in a silver coffin.

## 8. Matthew

"And Matthew wrote the Gospel in the Hebrew tongue, and published it at Jerusalem, and fell asleep at Hierees, a town of Parthia."[38]

Before his conversion, Matthew went by the name of Levi the son of Alphæus. Luke and Mark record that a publican named Levi was called as an apostle, but Matthew uses the name Matthew for the same story.[39] It may be that Matthew comes from the Greek

---

38. Hippolytus, *On the Twelve Apostles*, 255.
39. Luke 5:27, 29; Mark 2:14; Matthew 9:9.

word μαθητής [mathetes], or *disciple*, and is a cognomen taken by Levi sometime after his calling. A publican is a tax collector. This does not mean he was simply a clerk appointed by the Romans to write out tax receipts. It meant that he had paid a princely sum to the Roman government for the right to collect taxes. He paid up front, and then got to keep everything he collected for the next year. In other words, the man was fabulously wealthy. We seem to have the idea that the apostles were illiterate and poor men. Perhaps some were, but not Matthew. He knew how to read, write, and cipher. He probably helped the apostles quite a bit, both as a financial contributor and as a bookkeeper.

Although he does not play a prominent part in gospel accounts, Matthew was hugely important to early Christians because of the gospel he wrote. In fact, one early Christian community (the Ebionites, exclusively Jewish Christians) centered their doctrine on Matthew, rejecting the letters of Paul entirely.

What little anyone has conjectured about Matthew's later life and death is so mixed up and jumbled that it is pretty much worthless. Both Hippolytus and Heracleon, writing in the late second century, said that Matthew died a natural death.[40] But the official *Roman Martyrology*, published in the 1500s, says, "Matthew preached in Ethiopia and was killed there." African traditions claim that his manner of death ranges from burning to stoning to clubbing to beheading. Modern legends have his body being buried in a place called Naddaver somewhere in Ethiopia, but that place name is nowhere to be found nowadays. Somehow the relics got rediscovered and transported to Salerno, Italy (about fifty miles southwest of Naples), where they remain to this day. Since the deposition of Matthew's bones happened at about the same time that Bartholomew's remains arrived in nearby Benevento, I would say that their appearance was a way to keep Salerno's pilgrims spending their tourist shillings at home.

---

40. Clement of Alexandria, *Stromata*, 4.9. Scholars who reference this work say that the quote means Matthew did not die a martyr. The quote, however, is ambiguous. I knuckle under to peer pressure here because they are scholars. But I am not sure Heraclon says what they think he says.

## 9. James of Alphæus

"And James the son of Alphæus, when preaching in Jerusalem, was stoned to death by the Jews, and was buried there beside the temple."[41]

Welcome to the most controversial personality among the apostles. We have already met James the Greater, the son of Zebedee and brother of John. But the writers of the gospels included many more Jameses in their accounts, not taking any time to give helpful hints as to who they might have been referring to. I will not lead you through all the conjecture, because it is too confusing. Instead, as Inigo Montoya said, "Let me sum up."[42]

There are two other men named James: Jesus' brother and Jesus' cousin. Jerome (the man who first translated the LP&S and GE&A into Latin) thinks these two men are the same person. He believed that Jesus' mother, Mary, never had sexual relations. So when the evangelists write "the brother of Jesus," according to Jerome, brother was simply a way of saying cousin. Jesus had an uncle and aunt named Cleopas and Mary. Uncle Cleopas may have been the one on the road to Emmaus, and Aunt Mary may have been present at the crucifixion. Cleopas is actually just the Greek derivation of the Aramaic name Chalpai. The Latin derivation of that same name is Alphæus. Cleopas and Alphæus are the same person, and James was "of Alphæus." James "the Less" of Alphæus was Jesus' cousin, and can comfortably be conflated with James "the Just," something that Shelton says "is constant in both ancient writings and contemporary scholarship."[43] The Latter-day Saints, however, have no problem with Mary having produced other children, so the existence of a third James, the half-blood brother of Jesus, is possible. That leaves us with James the Great (John's brother), James the Less (Jesus' cousin), and James the Just (Jesus' little brother). This becomes important in chapter four when Peter tells Clement to write a letter to James in Jerusalem in around 67 CE, because James the Great died in 42 CE and James the Less in 62 CE. There had to be a surviving James in order for that letter to be written.

---

41. Hippolytus, *On the Twelve Apostles*, 255.

42. Reiner, *The Princess Bride*.

43. Shelton, *Quest*, 204. Shelton, however, does not believe James of Alphæus is Jesus' relative at all.

We do know that the James identified as Jesus' relative and also later called "the Just" became the first "bishop of Jerusalem." I make the case in a later chapter that instead of being a "bishop," he was what Latter-day Saints would recognize as the successor to first counselor in the first First Presidency after Zebedee's son James was killed. As the leader of the congregation there, when the Romans happened to be otherwise engaged (in 62 CE, according to Josephus), the Jewish Sanhedrin decided to lynch the leader of what were then called Nazarenes. This James the Just was first thrown from the "pinnacle of the temple" (probably the Golden Gate which descends precipitously to the Kidron Valley), but the fall did not kill him, so his assailants came down to finish the job with stones and at least one club, and then sawed his corpse into pieces. So if you see a depiction of an apostle with a saw or a club, that is James. Any relics belonging to him are said to be housed in the Cathedral of St. James in Jerusalem, in the same cathedral where James of Zebedee's head is preserved, although James the Lesser/Just's remains are supposedly under the high altar, which was where his home once stood. Yes, right on the same spot as James of Zebedee's execution, because that is what you do, build your house where your good friend died. Some fragments are said to have made their way to the Church of the Holy Apostles in Rome, although none of them have a provenance of earlier than the twelfth century when the cathedral was built in Jerusalem.

## 10. Simon

"Simon the Zealot, the son of Cleopas, who is also called Jude, became bishop of Jerusalem after James the Just, and fell asleep and was buried there at the age of 120 years."[44]

In the LDS general conference of October 2020, Elder Jeremy R. Jaggi gave an address on the virtue of patience. In this address he referenced Simon the Zealot. Since I was writing this book at that time, my ears perked right up, hoping for something new with which to populate this sparse little section. Jaggi pointed out that Zealots were associated with violence against both Romans and their Jewish collaborators. He goes on to say "Simon may have embraced and

---

44. Hippolytus, *On the Twelve Apostles*, 255.

advocated his philosophy with zeal and passion, but the scriptures suggest that through the influence and example of the Savior, his focus changed. His discipleship of Christ became the central focus of his life's efforts."[45] Elder Jaggi is not wrong; the GE&A does suggest that the focus of each apostle indeed changed. But there is no direct scriptural reference for any such metamorphosis experienced by Simon specifically.

Simon's identity is only slightly less controversial than James of Alphæus'. The difference between Matthew/Mark's identification of him as "the Canaanite" and Luke's calling him a Zealot is due to the Hebrew word *qanai*, meaning "zealous," being mistaken by some translators as meaning "Canaan." We believe the Bible to be the word of God as far as it is translated correctly, and here is an instance of a mistranslation. The question then arises, was Simon a Zealot like Judas Iscariot was? In first century CE Palestine, the word did not mean being overly faithful; it meant being vehemently opposed to Roman rule, to the point of taking up arms. If he was a Zealot, it is interesting that Jesus chose two of them to populate the Twelve.

Besides that murky hint at his political views, we are left with only conjecture about just who Simon was. In some extra-biblical traditions, he is associated with Mary Cleopas, Jesus' aunt who was listed as being at his crucifixion. But he also could have been one of Jesus' actual brothers. Whatever his relation to Jesus, it is interesting to note that Jesus was not averse to placing family members, whether brothers or cousins, in the Twelve. Perhaps it is a tacit tribute to the spiritual strength of Jesus' mortal family.

As for Simon's ministry and death, the traditions are so diverse that it is hard to credit them at all. He is said to have been the second bishop of the church in Jerusalem (we have at least two other contenders for that position) and to have suffered crucifixion there. Another tradition has him ending up in Britain where he was crucified on May 10, 61 CE. Or sawn in half in Persia. Or crucified in Samaria. Either the man was half cat with four or five lives, or people of various lands were fishing for some claim on an apostle's blood watering their homeland. Wherever he died, somehow some of his

---

45. Jeremy R. Jaggi, "Let Patience Have Her Perfect Work, and Count It All Joy!," *Ensign*, Nov. 2020.

relics have made their way to St. Peter's Basilica, where they are entombed in an altar dedicated to Jesus' foster father, Joseph.

## 11. Thaddeus — Judas

"Jude, who is also called Lebbæus, preached to the people of Edessa, and to all Mesopotamia, and fell asleep at Berytus (Beirut), and was buried there."[46]

"Edessa, and all the countries round about it which were on all sides of it, and Zoba, and Arabia, and all the north, and the regions round about it, and the south, and all the regions on the borders of Mesopotamia, received the apostles' ordination to the priesthood from Addæus the apostle, one of the seventy-two apostles, who himself made disciples there, and built a church there, and was priest and ministered there in his office of Guide which he held there."[47]

The identity of the eleventh apostle is so hopelessly jumbled that it is barely worth trying to make sense of it. In the end, one feels no surer of any one story than any other. This slot is filled with two completely separate identities: Thaddeus and Judas. The easiest solution is that *Thaddeus* is simply a miscopying of *Theudas*, which is the equivalent of Judas.[48] Some scholars contend that the name of Judas was so tainted by Iscariot, that Mark and Matthew used a completely different name. After all, Simon was known as Peter, so why couldn't Judas (not Iscariot) have the nickname Thaddeus? Most scholars, however, dismiss this notion, claiming instead that the original eleventh apostle either died or apostatized at some point prior to Pentecost. Perhaps not everyone was cut out for the job. Leaving home, family, livelihood, and crisscrossing Palestine may have led to dismissal or replacement.[49] More confusion enters the picture when we realize that one of the seventy's names was Thaddeus. Traditions of this man's ministry stretch into Edessa, including a story of a King Abgar who had heard of Jesus while he was yet alive and requested an audience or some other token. Jesus wiped his face with a towel and sent a Thaddeus to carry it to Abgar. Upon

---

46. Hippolytus, *On the Twelve Apostles*, 255.
47. Anonymous, *The Teaching of the Apostles*, 671.
48. Brownrigg, *The Twelve Apostles*, 161.
49. Meier, "The Circle of the Twelve," 635–72.

receiving it, Abgar was miraculously healed, causing the conversion of his entire kingdom. The story, however, is of at least third century CE derivation. In 1967 a pair of archaeologists reported unearthing an ossuary that was labeled "Judas Thaddeus" that dates to at least the second century CE, but no other context relates it to the apostle. The identity of Thaddeus, then, is completely dark.

Judas also has some confusing references to dig through. Jesus had a brother named Judas, identified in both Matthew and Mark. The name Jude is simply a shortening of Judas, like Rob for Robert, so the author of the Epistle of Jude is also a Judas. Catholic tradition states that both these Judases are the same person, but Protestants are unconvinced. Luke mentions a "Jude of James" in Luke and Acts, but no one is sure whether he is James's son or James's brother, nor who the heck James is. Big-tent Catholics think these Judases are one and the same with Mark's Judas and the author of Jude, while Protestants think otherwise. No one knows which is right, as there is absolutely no solid evidence to correlate or differentiate the various Judases. All we know for certain is that he was not Judas Iscariot.

A less trustworthy tradition contends that he was killed with Simon the Zealot in Beirut (yet another death for poor Simon), but this tradition dates to at least the third century CE. He was said to have been killed with an axe, thus making him a victim of decapitation. Some believe his remains traveled some 2,000 miles eastward to Kyrgyzstan, while others contend that they were brought directly from Beirut to Rome where they can be venerated along with Simon the Zealot's bones. But the more accepted account of Thaddeus Lebbæus Judas's passing is that he died of illness.[50]

## 12. Judas Iscariot

While some bandy about the theory that Judas's surname, *Iscariot*, derives from a band of assassins known as the *Sicarii*, this would make the man a time traveler, because scholars agree that the group did not arise until at least a decade after the Crucifixion.[51] More probably it is just a name inserted by the gospel writers to differentiate

---

50. Hippolytus, *On the Twelve Apostles*, 255; Anonymous, *Teaching of Addaeus the Apostle*, 657–69.

51. Brown, *Death of the Messiah*, 688–92; Meier, *A Marginal Jew*, 210.

between him and Judas Thaddeus, and was likely the name of the town from which he hailed. John accuses Iscariot of embezzling the Twelve's money, but does not offer any substantiating details (D&C 135:7; John 13:27–30). What Iscariot did, why, and what became of him afterward are matters of endless conjecture because he did not offer up a convenient monologue as in modern crime novels. Since there are no reliable sources, conjectures from across the belief spectrum, even from luminaries like C. S. Lewis and Bart Ehrman, lead to no definitive ends.[52]

The apocryphal *Story of Joseph of Arimathaea* attempts to fill out the story surrounding Jesus' arrest and crucifixion from a Jewish point of view. First, it gives the names and crimes of the two thieves who were punished alongside Jesus: Gestas and Demas. The former was a brigand who murdered and mutilated travelers, while the latter at least robbed from the rich to give to the poor. His most recent heist had targeted some special portion of the temple treasury. Judas, who had been put on the rather paltry retainer of a golden didrachma per day to spy on Jesus, suggested that Jesus be blamed for the temple theft, but Nicodemus and Caiaphas's daughter felt that Jesus' declaration that he could destroy the temple was treasonous enough.[53] This account can be easily dismissed on several matters of internal error. First, didrachmas were never made of gold. Second, the presence of a woman in a council of the Sanhedrin is implausible. And finally, that Nicodemus alone should be named among the Sanhedrin is rather convenient. The thieves' names and crimes were standard bogeymen in post-primitive literature.

Another apocryphal work that mentions Judas is the *Acts of Thomas*. It admits that while adultery is the worst sin, theft brought on by the covetousness that plagued Iscariot is next on the list.[54] The pseudepigraphal *Book of the Resurrection of Christ*, attributed to Bartholomew, depicts Jesus' visit to hell where he "delivered Adam and the holy souls, then turned to Judas Iscariot and uttered a long

---

52. Christensen, *C. S. Lewis on Scripture*, Appendix A. Bart Ehrman, "Can We Know Anything Historically about How Judas Iscariot Died?," The Bart Ehrman Blog, Apr. 3, 2020, https://ehrmanblog.org.

53. Rhodes, "Acts of Andrew," 161–62.

54. Rhodes, "Acts of Andrew," 402.

rebuke, and described the sufferings which he must endure. Thirty names of sins are given."[55]

### 13. Paul of Tarsus

You will note that I have skipped apostle no. 13—Matthias. This is not because I suffer from triskaidekaphobia, but because he is outside the scope of the original Twelve. Neither is Paul listed among the original Twelve. For all we know, Paul may not even have been the fourteenth apostle. Was Barnabas a member of the Twelve? Was he not senior to Paul? However, since Paul as yet holds the title of being, according to many sources, the man who has done more, save Jesus only, for the salvation of men in the world, we add him to this list (D&C 135:3).[56]

Paul's story is documented in great detail in the Acts of the Apostles. We know of his wide travels and his disputes with the rest of the Twelve about whether non-Judean converts should adhere to the Mosaic Law. His attitude toward "gentiles" got him in hot water with the Jewish leadership at the temple and led to his seeking protection from Roman authorities, which, after several years, led him to make an appeal to be tried in Rome. Luke faithfully records Paul's voyage to Rome and his kind treatment by its authorities, but we have no account of his demise in the scriptures. A close reading of Paul's letters to Timothy indicates that he was released from his Roman captivity and made at least one more journey that started in Crete, bounced along the Dalmatian Coast, made at least three stops in Greece, and then returned to Rome. Clement opens up the possibility that Paul journeyed to Spain, saying that Paul was "a teacher of righteousness unto the whole world" who had "reached the furthest bounds of the West and bore testimony before the ruling powers."[57] We should be aware that most modern scholars dismiss the writings of Clement and the letters of Paul to Timo-

---

55. Rhodes, "Acts of Andrew," 183.

56. Steven Skiena and Charles B. Ward, "Who's Biggest? The 100 Most Significant Figures in History," *Time*, Dec. 10, 2013. I personally believe Joseph Smith will be recognized as holding the honor arrogated to him by John Taylor, but in the meantime, computational data-centric analysis puts Paul a good twenty places in front of him.

57. Lightfoot and Harmer, *Biblical Essays*, 423.

thy and Titus as being, at worst, first-century forgeries and, at best, historical fiction—similar to Gerald Lund's imaginative retelling of LDS history, *The Work and the Glory*. I address this in chapter four. However, it is difficult to correlate the dates of Paul's house arrest (60–63 CE) with his death in Rome at the same time as Peter's (68 CE) without the intervening journeys.[58]

There are traditions that say he was held in chains along with Peter in the Mamertine Prison that still stands at the western edge of the Imperial Forum in Rome. Those traditions also say that when he was beheaded, his head bounced three times, and that at each spot it bounced a fountain burst from the ground.[59] The spot is marked today by the Abbey of Three Fountains and the Church of St. Paul at the Three Fountains, which are a forty-five-minute metro ride from downtown in Rome. Since these monuments do not date back further than the fifth century CE, their authenticity can be somewhat doubted. However, Paul's burial place, like Peter's, is of very ancient derivation. The Basilica of Saint Paul Outside the Walls is a quick fifteen-minute metro ride from the Colosseum and even has its own stop. The same Gaius who set up Peter's memorial claimed to have been able to point out Paul's burial place on the road to Ostia in a Roman cemetery. Paul, being a Roman citizen, was entitled to the quick death of decapitation and proper burial in a cemetery, both of which had been denied to Peter. The same Constantine who commissioned the first Basilica of St. Peter also authorized Paul's Basilica, transferring his headless corpse into a properly magnificent sarcophagus, which is still present at the site. My LDS post-mission tour to Rome did not include a stop at Paul's resting place, but I was able to crane my neck to see the supposed resting place of his head, marked by a magnificent structure, called a baldachin, over the high altar in the more centrally located Lateran Arch-Cathedral where it shares a place in a golden bust next to a bust of Peter that is said to contain at least parts of Peter's skull.[60] The Roman Church uses its possession of these relics to bolster its claim to the true apostolic succession.

---

58. Eusebius, *Church History*, 2.25.5.

59. Lanzi and Lanzi, *Saints and Their Symbols*, 61.

60. While most people think that the Vatican has been the headquarters of the Roman Church over the millennia, St. John Lateran Arch-Cathedral has been the church's headquarters since the fourth century. The Pope made his move to the Vatican around

## Summary

We have come to the end of the facts, legends, and traditions of the lives and fates of the original twelve apostles. As you can see, much of what is currently held as fact about what happened to the various members of the Twelve is so convoluted, confusing, and fanciful as to be almost totally without merit. While early and strong documentation exists for the martyrdom of James, Peter, and Paul, any evidence of what happened to the other Twelve is late and mostly apocryphal. The stories of the passing of John, Matthew, and Judas Thaddeus show that at least a quarter of the Twelve were not martyrs, which at the very least disproves this first myth that "all the apostles died as martyrs." There is neither doctrinal nor textual proof of all the Twelve sealing their testimony with their blood.

However, by almost all the accounts, the Twelve went to more parts of the known world than I had previously supposed. They probably visited the Middle East, southern Europe, Turkey, and even Persia and India. Perhaps even Africa and Britannia.

---

the sixteenth century, but his Episcopal seat is still in the apse of St. John Lateran Arch-Cathedral.

MYTH 2

# PETER WAS NOT THE FIRST POPE

In just about every film adaptation of Jesus' ministry I have seen, from the *Greatest Story Ever Told* to the videos produced by the LDS Church, the characters deliver their invariably stilted Shakespearean English lines in a most solemn of manners. Not only that, but for some reason, Jesus has an English accent. Yes, Jesus was the Son of God, and he should be treated with the utmost respect. But come on, if the man never even smiled, would you want to hang around him all the time? Every holy man I have known has had a sense of when to be solemn and when to crack a good joke.

If I were a filmmaker, my depiction of Jesus appearing to the apostles in the closed room after the resurrection would go something like this: In an effort to put the apostles at ease, Jesus asks for some food so that he can eat it and prove he is not a ghost. Some poor apostle, let's say Bartholomew, gets the nod from Peter, picks up a fish sandwich, and proffers it to Jesus—very much keeping his distance. Bartholomew is shaking so badly that the handoff results in the food tumbling to the floor. All the apostles back away. "See, it *is* a ghost," their frightened expressions say. Jesus, trying to protect Bartholomew's pride and deflate the terror of the situation, leans over and picks up the sandwich. "Heh, heh," he chuckles, "first day with my new hands."

Yes, I know, it's a joke from the 1990s and there was no such thing as a sandwich in Jesus' time. But in my mind, it is both funny and illustrative. No doctrine is changed, nothing about Jesus' character is demeaned, and we can all better internalize the drama of the moment.

In that vein, like LDS Apostle Jeffrey Holland, I would like to "ask your indulgence as I take some non-scriptural liberty in my portrayal" of the story of Peter getting his nickname.[1] You may compare it with Matthew 16:13–19.

Shortly after the events on the Mount of Transfiguration, Jesus sat down with his apostles and asked them, "So, what is the rumor mill saying about my identity?" They reported several theories that were getting tossed around the community, but apparently Jesus sensed a little anxiety in their answers. "Okay, that's what *they* say about me, but tell me, what do *you* think? Who am I?" Perhaps James or Judas offered some half-hearted replies, but the only answer that got Jesus' attention was Simon's: "You are the Anointed One, the son of the Living God" (Matt. 16:18).

Jesus, the master teacher, did not just give the man a well-deserved fist bump, he found a way to turn this into a teaching moment. First, he called the apostle by his full name, much like our mothers called us by our full names when they wanted our undivided attention: "Simon, son of Jonah." (This was important, because Jesus was about to give him a different name.) "You aren't convinced one way or the other by what the rumors say, but you believe what you yourself have witnessed." We should point out at this point that Simon later displays a definite character flaw: waffling. Remember when Peter pledges his undying loyalty to Jesus and then denies him three times? But at this moment, Simon believed—and he was willing to lay it on the line and say so. Jesus knew that, like the alcoholic who forswears drinking but will most likely have relapses down the road, Simon might not be as steadfast in the future as he was at this moment. So he put his arm around the man, looked him in the eye, and said "You, my friend, are a ROCK."

One arm still around Simon, Jesus used his other hand to point at him and said to the other apostles, "And this is the rock I'm going to use as the foundation for my synagogue." He specifically chose a word that described both Simon's devotion and the foundation of all enduring buildings: rock. And from that point onward, Jesus called Simon "Peter," to remind both Simon and the other apostles of Simon's faith in this moment.

In case you do not know how we get from rock to Peter, here is

---

1. Jeffrey R. Holland, "The First Great Commandment," *Ensign*, Nov. 2020.

the roadmap. Jesus did not actually say rock, as that is an English word. The Aramaic word he used is pronounced *keefa*, a word you might see elsewhere in the GE&A as Cephas but probably heard mispronounced as *seefas* instead of the Aramaic *keefas*. Although Matthew may have indeed written his gospel in Hebrew and used *keefa*, when it was translated into Greek, the word was rendered *petros*, which eventually morphed into the English *Peter*.

You may have noticed that, in my little story, I took the liberty of saying synagogue instead of church. I chose that word because the apostles, who were having enough difficulty recognizing Jesus' identity, did not have a clue about what a church was. Jesus likely used the Aramaic word that described both the gathering of people and the building they gathered to, a word that comes down to us in Greek as *synagogue*, or gathering.

Now we come back to "upon Petros I will build my church," because I can hear some of you saying, "Whoa, back up the bus. Peter is not the rock. Joseph Smith said 'the rock of *revelation*.'" Yes, I have heard it too—even taught it to many an investigator on my mission. B. H. Roberts is insistent that if Jesus meant that Peter was the intended foundation stone, he would have said "upon thee" and not "upon this rock."[2] He claims that by saying "rock" Jesus was referring to the principle of revelation. There are, however, a couple of prickly problems with this idea.

The first is that Joseph Smith never said it. He was talking once about John baptizing Jesus and, in a sidebar, quotes the second half of Matthew 16:18 and then says "What rock? Revelation."[3] Then he goes right back to the subject of baptism. The phrase "rock of revelation" was not coined until thirty years later when George Q. Cannon was talking about Catholics' vs. Protestants' claims about the papacy and said, "What rock? The rock of revelation—the principle upon which he was talking."[4] It was Cannon, not Smith, who developed this concept.

Further, if Jesus was hoping to convince the apostles that revelation would guide the church, as demonstrated by Simon's revelation,

---

2. Roberts, *Outlines of Ecclesiastical History*, 160.

3. Smith Jr. et al., 5:258.

4. George Q. Cannon, "Persecution—First Principles—Priesthood," June 11, 1871, *Journal of Discourses*, 26 vols. (Liverpool: Latter-day Saints' Book Depot, 1854–86), 14:171.

then why would he allude to revelation as a rock? Nowhere in the LP&S is there an allusion to revelation being a rock. Jesus frequently used existing scriptural devices, like quotes and stories, to help his listeners understand gospel concepts, but "revelation is a rock" had no scriptural precedent. It would be as if today someone said, "Linda, you really understand the secret of compound interest. As a matter of fact, I'm going to call you Penny from now on. Everyone, this is the penny of success that you need to build your portfolios on." In our culture, there is no such concept as a penny of success. A key to success? Yes, we know that one. But a penny? That is how odd the concept "rock of revelation" would have sounded to Jesus' apostles.

The point I'm trying to make is that, contrary to the argument that we and our Protestant friends have been making for more than five centuries, Jesus *was* referring to Peter when he said "upon this rock." The Catholic Church believes that Peter was given the keys to the kingdom, and, further, that the keys have been passed on through an unbroken line of leaders to today's pope. The early Protestants (not just Luther and his followers, but many before and concurrent with them) saw the contemporary popes as lacking actual priesthood power, and so tried to throw out the baby with the bathwater by denying that the office of the Bishop of Rome *ever* had any superseding priesthood authority. William of Ockham (yes, the Occam's razor guy, despite the different spelling) got the ball rolling in the thirteenth century CE when he was excommunicated for disagreeing with the pope about how much money the clergy should control.[5] John Wyclif called the papacy and the begging monks in fourteenth-century England nothing less than the anti-Christ.[6] Jan Hus, who inherited Wyclif's mantle in Bohemia (the modern-day Czech Republic), condemned the papal sale of indulgences to finance a war. Hus proclaimed that no church leader had the right to draw the sword in the name of the church, but should rather use spiritual tactics—a proclamation for which he was burned at the stake.[7] Then Martin Luther, of course, lit the Reformation match that brought the house down while Pope Leo X was building a new

---

5. Robinson, *William of Ockham's Early Theory of Property Rights*, 32.
6. Lahey, *John Wyclif,* 193–94.
7. Dallmann, *John Hus,* 118.

headquarters for the church in Rome. The Latter-day Saints have inherited the Protestants' prejudice, even going so far as to associate Nephi's "great and abominable church" with the church at Rome.[8]

One more example of how religious scholars have militated against Peter's role as the rock may be illustrated by a citation from Cyrus Scofield's famous Bible commentary from the early twentieth century. Much may be gleaned from Scofield's scholarship and erudition, but in this case, he got it embarrassingly wrong. In his footnote to Matthew 16:18, he writes:

There is in the Greek a play upon the words, "thou art Peter [petros—literally 'a little rock'], and upon this rock [Petra] I will build my church." He does not promise to build His church upon Peter, but upon Himself, as Peter is careful to tell us (1 Pet. 2:4–9).[9]

Scofield's problem is that he is trying to differentiate between petros and petra *in Greek*. But Jesus did not speak in Greek to Peter. He spoke Aramaic and called him *keefas*. We have absolutely no idea whether he said rock, little rock, stone, or pebble. And from the teensy bit of Greek I know, the inflected difference between πετροσ and πετρα bends more toward grammar than vocabulary.

When we interpret Matthew 16 as referring to the rock of revelation, rather than to Peter, we unwittingly follow an early Protestant doctrine they projected back to Jesus' time in order to make their arguments against the current papacy. And by parroting these Protestant claims, we are actually denying one of our LDS beliefs, namely, that Peter was indeed given the keys to the kingdom, and that he and James and John constituted the first First Presidency. The primitive church was meant to be built upon the foundation of Peter's presidency every bit as much as the restored LDS Church was meant to be built upon the foundation of Joseph Smith's presidency. It is true that we do not believe that those keys were transmitted in their fullness from Peter to the modern pope (because of the intervening apostasy), but we do not need to deny flatly that Jesus intended Peter to lead the church and then come up with some questionable turn of phrase to redirect the Lord's quote.

Fair warning: I am now going to try to convince you that Peter

---

8. McConkie, *Mormon Doctrine*, 129–31.

9. Scofield and English, *The New Scofield Reference Bible*, Matt. 16:18.

was indeed the first pope. I know, even the proposition may set the teeth of some of you on edge, but please bear with me for a couple of paragraphs.

First, we should talk about the word "pope." What does it mean? As you might be aware, it is a form of the Latin word *papa*, or father. Many churches have a tradition of calling the person who leads a congregation some form of the word father. Priests in Catholic, Orthodox, and Episcopalian churches (as well as many, many others) go by the title of father. Colonel Potter of *M\*A\*S\*H* called Francis Mulcahy, his unit's Catholic chaplain, *padre*—Spanish for father. The head of a monastery is called the abbot, which is the Latinization of the word *abba*, meaning daddy or father. Interestingly, the head of a nunnery is called an abbess, which is the feminine form of father. Even the Latter-day Saints have a Primary song that the children sing on Father's Day that talks about "the father of our ward." It's a strange tradition considering Matthew 23:9, which reads: "Call no man your father upon the earth: for one is your Father, which is in heaven."

Returning to the pope, his title is just a way of saying *father* out of respect. But since the papa in Rome is the big cheese, he gets to be called *the* papa, or The Pope—the same way today's Latter-day Saints refer to our current head prophet, seer, and revelator as the Prophet, and Joseph Smith as The Prophet.

How is it that today's pope is connected with Peter? Catholics will say that Peter was the first bishop of Rome, though the term *bishop* was not invented until long after Peter had died. The word used to describe his office at the time was επίσκοπος [episcopos], literally *overseer*.[10] Peter was simply the one in charge in Rome. But since he was also the holder of the keys, his bishopric superseded every other bishopric, making him the head priest, the highest-ranking father, and thus the pope. Let us look at history and see how that bears out.

We read in Acts that, around 42 CE, King Herod had Peter and James imprisoned while the Romans were looking the other way (Acts 12:1–17). James was taken out first and run through with a sword, which got Herod such positive reviews from the Sanhedrin that he was gearing up to do the same to Peter. This is when an

---

10. Since the word is associated with American slavery, I use the Latin-derived equivalent: supervisor.

angel came, put the guards to sleep, and unlocked the doors, allowing Peter to escape. He headed to the home of a certain Mary and,
after finally getting a girl named Rhoda to let him in, told Mary to
let the rest of the brethren know that he had escaped. Then, before
the guards could awaken and sound the alarm, "he departed, and
went into another place." We do not know where that other place
was, but it might have been Rome, and Luke might have left out
the name of that city to avoid giving the authorities information
about an escaped convict.[11] Curiously enough, another very early
document of the post-primitive church gives the number of years of
Peter's "papacy" as being about twenty-five, which, when added to
42 CE, would put his death right about 67 CE when Nero is supposed to have executed him. This would give Peter a very long time
to establish a functioning church in Rome—a central point from
which to coordinate the preaching of the gospel to "all the world."
Basically, he served as what Latter-day Saints would call today an
area president. Certainly, Peter did not stay in Rome the entire time.
We know he attended a church conference in Jerusalem around 49
CE, and there are hints of him traveling to other locations—even
taking Mrs. Peter with him.

The length of Peter's papacy is documented in a book called the
*Liber Pontificalis* (Book of Popes), a history of the popes dating to
the beginning of the church. Most scholars doubt the authenticity
of much of what is recorded in the book because the records can
only be reliably dated back to the fourth or fifth century CE. However, upon reading the first entries in the section about Peter, I was
impressed with its congruity with what a Latter-day Saint would
expect of the organization and perpetuation of the church.

For example, *Liber* lists the names of several men who served as
supervisors along with Peter, including Linus, Cletus, and Clement.
Modern Catholic opinion does not support the idea of concurrent
supervisors, and instead goes to great lengths to make Linus and Cletus successors to the blessed Saint Peter, leaving Clement out entirely.
*Liber*, however, says that Peter "ordained two bishops, Linus and Cletus, who in person fulfilled all the services of the priest in the city of

---

11. Wenham, "Did Peter Go to Rome in AD 42?," 95.

Rome for the inhabitants and for strangers; then the blessed Peter gave himself to prayer and preaching, instructing the people."[12] They seemed to be bishops serving concurrently with Peter. To a Latter-day Saint, it looks like they were given charge of temporal affairs of the city while Peter maintained the spiritual affairs of the church—much along the modern lines of local leader vs. general authority.

Was Peter the first pope as depicted in some fanciful Renaissance portraits? Obviously not. I do, however, believe there is enough evidence to support the claim that Peter was the highest priesthood authority in Rome as well as the senior apostle. To say that he was a "bishop" is anachronistic, seeing as how the title did not even exist in his time, but that he was "supervisor" is quite acceptable. There is a documented succession of leaders of the church in Rome from the very beginning. Whether those leaders were called supervisors, bishops, fathers, or popes, there is a relatively unbroken line of succession from Peter to Francis. With those ducks in a row, perhaps one may at least sigh and admit that Peter was indeed the first leader in a long line of succession that eventually ended up as the modern papacy.

---

12. Anonymous, *Liber Pontificalis*, 4–6.

# MYTH 3

# THE PRIESTHOOD WAS TAKEN
# FROM THE EARTH

One day, while working in the temple, I was having a discussion with one of my fellow workers about the great apostasy and asked him when he thought the priesthood was taken from the Earth. He said he thought that on the day the Apostle Peter died, or when the last apostle died (he was not sure which), the priesthood authority of every other bishop, seventy, teacher, and deacon immediately ceased. Intrigued, I asked whether *his* priesthood authority would cease when the prophet died. "Of course not," he replied, "the Quorum of Twelve still holds all the keys." I agreed, but then queried what might happen if a jetliner crashed into the Salt Lake City LDS Conference Center during the Sunday morning session of general conference and suddenly all fifteen prophets, seers, and revelators were suddenly taken from the Earth? What would happen to his authority? He stuck with his original opinion and responded that his authority would indeed immediately cease. The bell then rang for the next session and our discussion ended.

It is an interesting opinion—that the priesthood ceased immediately after the last apostle died. But there is a problem either way you look at it. First, most Latter-day Saints believe that John never died, which would mean that the priesthood was never taken. But, for argument's sake, let us leave John out of it and go by the day Thomas died in far-off India. There were an awful lot of men (and women, I might add) who were ministering in other parts of the world without knowing that the last leaf had fallen from the apostolic tree. Did they suddenly cease to get inspiration? Were their ordinances and blessings suddenly null and void?

LDS authors from James E. Talmage to Kent P. Jackson share my colleague's opinion: The priesthood evaporated upon the death of the apostles. Talmage says, "Nor is there record of any ordination of individuals to the apostleship ... beyond those whose calling and ministry are chronicled in the New Testament, which, as a historical record, ends with the first century."[1] B. H. Roberts opines that since "men were rapidly proving themselves unworthy of the Church of Christ, the Lord did not permit his servants to perpetuate these quorums of the higher priesthood."[2] Hugh Nibley affirms that Jesus' Matthew 24 reference to "the end" referred not to the end of the world, but to the end of the dispensation, which would come when the last apostle died.[3] And Jackson echoes "When [John] left his public ministry around A.D. 100, apostleship ceased, and the keys of the kingdom were taken."[4]

I would like to go to bat against these noteworthy pitchers.

However, in this chapter, I am not going to be talking about the apostleship, or the higher priesthood, or the keys to the kingdom. I am going to be talking about the priesthood we Saints believe was held by about 99 percent of members of the church: anything *other* than the office of apostle. We will deal with the heavy pitching in the next chapter where I consider whether Peter had a chance to pass on his priesthood keys before his death, thus extending the apostleship for another generation.

We do not have the slightest chance of knowing at what date the remaining 99 percent of the priesthood was taken from the earth. Except for intellectually oriented nerds like me, who even cares? Instead, I will try to demonstrate that the priesthood hung around for a lot longer than we might think. In fact, I am going to suggest that the priesthood was not taken from the Earth at all. Rather, in keeping with LDS belief, it gradually dried up. There is a huge difference.

There is an old trope about a child who, when the game does not go his way, says "Fine, I'll just take my ball and go home!" This is not the mature way to handle a situation. But when we say that "the

---

1. Talmage, *Great Apostasy*, 172–73.
2. Roberts, *Outlines of Ecclesiastical History*, 151.
3. Nibley, *Passing of the Church*, 2.
4. Jackson, *From Apostasy to Restoration*, 19.

priesthood was taken from the Earth," we are basically saying that when the apostles got killed, God, in effect, said, "Fine, I'll just take my priesthood and go home!" It seems strange, considering what we know of his character, to think that the Lord would not do everything he could to save every last soul before priesthood authority dwindled down to nothing. To imagine that at some point he said, "We are done," and somehow withdrew the power being exercised in his name seems, in my opinion, ludicrous.

"But you're just playing with words," you may say. "Whether priesthood power was taken or whether it died out really doesn't make any difference. It was still gone in the end." I grant that the end result is the same, but finding out how long it took to reach the end gives us a better idea of how the great apostasy actually came about, and to what extent it affects today's LDS Church.

Let us start with the argument of my temple-working friend. I do not believe that God's priesthood is like a creature whose body immediately dies if its head is cut off. The argument that follows reflects my understanding of LDS teaching. Although priesthood *authority* can only be distributed by authorized personnel, priesthood *power* is something that one personally cultivates and retains, based on the keeping of covenants.[5] Were the head of the church to be cut off, the authority to name *new* general officers, stake leaders, and ward bishops would certainly be curtailed, but the authority already given to the current leaders would not expire until they were released or died. Hence, were some apocalypse to come about that annihilated the general leadership but spared my stake president and bishop, those men would still be authorized to continue issuing temple recommends, setting apart quorum presidencies, and leading the wards under their supervision. And since there was no authority to release them, they would continue to be authorized until they died.

This procedure was actually established by Clement of Rome in his *Epistle to the Corinthians*,

Our apostles also knew, through our Lord Jesus Christ, that there would be strife on account of the office of the episcopate. For this reason, therefore, inasmuch as they had obtained a perfect foreknowledge of this,

---

5. Boyd K. Packer, "The Power of the Priesthood," *Ensign*, May 2010.

they appointed those [ministers] already mentioned, and afterwards gave instructions, that when these should fall asleep, other approved men should succeed them in their ministry. We are of opinion, therefore, that those appointed by them, or afterwards by other eminent men, with the consent of the whole church, and who have blamelessly served the flock of Christ, in a humble, peaceable, and disinterested spirit, and have for a long time possessed the good opinion of all, cannot be justly dismissed from the ministry.[6]

In other words, Clement not only says that the apostles gave instructions for how to perpetuate the priesthood, but that those who held offices could not be dismissed without good reason.

If we conjecture that the priesthood was withdrawn wholesale from the Earth after the death of the apostles (except, of course, for John's), then the priesthood would have been extinct by 100 CE. This date is assuming that one of the Twelve might have been as young as twenty when he answered Jesus' call to the ministry between 25 and 30 CE. Even if he survived to be an octogenarian (pretty long in the tooth for men of those days), he still would have died before the turn of the second century CE. So we can safely assume that eleven of the original Twelve were pushing up daisies by 100 CE. But we would be wrong to assume that tucked in their coffins was a copy of their priesthood lines of authority with the last line reading "The End."

Let me show you what I mean. Eusebius recorded that, sometime in the 90s CE, John ordained a thirty-something-year-old man named Polycarp (meaning "very fruitful") to the office of supervisor.[7] Polycarp lived another sixty years after that—his rather brutal death being documented in 155 CE.[8] At the time of his death, he was honored for being a marvelously faithful and considerate man. He had, after all, sixty years of service to the Lord under his belt. Polycarp's case shows that priesthood authorization endures independently of its authorizer. But what about Polycarp's ability to propagate *his* priesthood?

If the post-primitive church followed the modern precedent of LDS stake presidents and bishops needing to be authorized by

---

6. Clement of Rome, *Epistle to the Corinthians*, 242.
7. Eusebius, *Church History*, 3.36.1.
8. Eusebius, *Church History*, 4.15.1–48.

apostles, Polycarp could not have designated his own successor. However, modern LDS priesthood leaders *are* authorized to ordain new elders, priests, teachers, and deacons, along with organizing and leading the church in their geographic area—all without having to get approval from Salt Lake City. Likewise, up until 155 CE, Polycarp may have appropriately authorized the ordination of new elders. Let us call one of them Fortunatus, who was then in his mid-twenties. Fortunatus might live until the turn of the third century when he might have ordained one of his grandsons, we'll call him Gaius, as a priest. Gaius might have lived until 250 CE and might have, in turn, ordained one of his grandsons, little Septimius, a deacon, who might have survived until the turn of the fourth century. This scenario more than triples the time during which authorized priesthood holders could at least preach, teach, expound, and exhort, even according to our own modern LDS definitions of priesthood offices and duties.

Did every authorized priesthood officer live a life as exemplary as Polycarp? No. In fact, some ventured out to claim new or unauthorized positions. For example, we have record of the Ebionites, a collection of saints from the heartland of Judea who moved out into the country away from the mainstream church—as evidenced by their rejection of gentile (non-Jewish) converts, their editing of the Gospel of Matthew, and their rejection of Paul's epistles. We discuss movements such as these in chapter five, but for the moment we acknowledge that not all priesthood ordinations resulted in the exercise and/or perpetuation of real priesthood power.

We must admit, though, that effective and righteous priesthood power could have remained and been perpetuated by good and faithful women and men for a century or two past the time the apostles' ministry ceased. God would not have revoked their power and authority; their upstream link would have merely perished. I imagine that God was disappointed that he could not function through a living church like our own—one that had the keys to perpetuate itself. But can you imagine a God who would throw up his hands, take his priesthood ball, and go home?

Here is another possibility to explore. Did the primitive apostles have authorization to appoint their own successors, instead of having to meet as a quorum to get unanimous agreement on a new apostle? In other words, did the original Twelve have a set of operating instructions different from ours?

The LDS authors who have written about the great apostasy assumed that the Lord's primitive church operated the same way the Lord's current church does. There is, however, no ancient documentation supporting this view. In fact, we have a scriptural record that shows, at the very least, that the selection process of a primitive apostle differed significantly from our modern process.

Several months after Judas Iscariot's death, the church met to fill his vacant spot in the Twelve (Acts 1:15–16). In a conference that consisted of not just the remaining eleven apostles, but of 120 brethren, the names of two men, Joseph "Barsabus" Justus and Matthias, were presented to fill the vacancy. The whole conference then prayed and cast lots, the result of which was their appointment of Matthias to the Twelve. Think about that. The whole conference cast votes between two men. The scriptures do not record whether the vote was unanimous or just a majority, but whatever the method or outcome, this is not the way apostolic callings are conducted in the modern church. These days, in the LDS Church, the Prophet/First Presidency selects the candidate, who is then ratified by the Quorum of Twelve. After ratification, the new apostle is ordained and later presented to the church in general conference for a sustaining vote. But, in this instance at least, the primitive church members chose among candidates.

Outside of biblical writings, there exists a great store of works that can give us more information on this topic. It is divided into two sets: apocryphal and patristic writings. The word apocryphal comes from the Greek αποκρυφοσ [apokrüfos] meaning *hidden*, and connoting "not approved for public consumption" in the Christian context. The word patristic comes from the Greek πατέρας [pateras] meaning *father*. The fathers being referenced are the eminent Christian writers of the period before 325 CE.

Among the apocryphal works are gospels, acts, and epistles attributed to various apostles. One of the most trusted of these is the *Didache* (pronounced *did-uh-kay).* The word simply means *teachings.* For many years, the *Didache* was known only through fragments quoted by Eusebius and other authors, but in 1873 a full copy, dating from 1056 CE, was discovered in Constantinople. Most modern scholars place the original work in at least the early first century CE.[9] A pair of LDS scholars has even moved it back as far as 70 CE.[10] In his massive work on apocryphal and patristic literature, Johannes Quasten notes that, because of the way the writing is organized, it could not have been written before 95 CE and that the document was later tampered with.[11] What we know is that the original text was composed during the living memory of those who had heard the apostles.

The *Didache*, then, is a source mostly trusted by both mainstream Christian and LDS scholars to give us a window into the very early post-primitive church. What does it have to say about how priesthood leaders might have been selected after the apostles were gone?

> Ordain for yourselves supervisors and servants of the church worthy of the Lord, meek, not lovers of money, truthful, and approved; for they too minister to you the ministry of the Prophets and Teachers. Therefore, do not despise your supervisors and servants of the church, for they are those that are the honored among you with the Prophets and Teachers.[12]

Apparently, supervisors were being sought out by congregation members, with righteousness as a top qualification. And while later tradition translates ἐπισκόπους as *bishop*, the term can apply to any position of leadership, including that of an apostolic successor. In other words, the post-primitive church had not gotten any memo from the apostles that they were supposed to stop filling leadership positions.

Eusebius tells us that when the spiritual supervisor of any great city died, the people voted on who should become his successor. Bishoprics are documented through at least the first half of the second century CE. When James the Just was killed in 62 CE, Eusebius records that Simeon held the office for the next forty-five years, followed by Justus for six years, and then Zacchaeus. After Zacchaeus, names continue to appear but without definite dates. Somehow this supervisory role continued in Jerusalem even though the city was

---

9. O'Loughlin, *The Didache*, 2.

10. Daniel C. Peterson and Stephen D. Ricks, "Comparing LDS Beliefs with First Century Christianity," *Ensign*, Mar. 1988.

11. Quasten, *Patrology*, 36.

12. Anonymous, *Didache*, 15.1–2. Translation my own.

destroyed in 70 CE. How were these successors appointed to office? Eusebius records that after Anterus, the leader of the church at Rome, died in 236 CE, "all the brethren had assembled to select by vote him who should succeed to the supervision of the church."[13] A man named Fabianus came to the assembly from outside Rome and was on no one's list of supervisor candidates. However, when a dove descended and sat upon Fabianus' shoulder, it was taken as a sign that he should be appointed, making Fabianus the twentieth leader of the church at Rome. The dove descending was something new and remarkable, but the fact that the elders met to elect a new supervisor needed no explanation, it being as mundane as Dad picking who would say grace at dinner.

The modern Catholic Church acknowledges Fabianus as the twentieth pope, but very few Latter-day Saints are prepared to admit that he was a legitimate successor to Peter since we tend to contend that God had withdrawn the priesthood from the earth a century and a half before Fabianus was elected. Remember, however, that among the brethren assembled to select who should succeed Anterus there were very probably men living who had been rightfully ordained deacons by someone who had rightfully been ordained a priest by a bishop who had been ordained by an apostle. They followed an example that had been set forth in Peter's calling of Matthias. So we cannot say with certainty that Fabianus had no priesthood authority. Just as with the Nephite church in 250 CE in the Book of Mormon, there still could have been people legitimately authorized to conduct church business.

What difference does it make to the typical Latter-day Saint whether the priesthood was lost in 100 CE versus 250 CE—or even later? Perhaps very little. But in our discussions with members of other denominations, we might come off as a little less judgmental of their religious traditions if we were to say something like "the church up to that time had remained a pure and uncorrupted virgin, but when the sacred college of apostles had died and the generation of those that had been deemed worthy to hear the inspired wisdom with their own ears had passed away, then the league of

---

13. Eusebius, *Church History*, 6.29.3.

godless error took its rise as a result of the folly of heretical teachers, who, because none of the apostles was still living, attempted henceforth to proclaim the 'knowledge that is falsely so-called.'"[14] After all, this is what Hegesippus wrote in the late second century CE, and Hegesippus is regarded as a saint by the Roman Church. We would be quoting a member of the post-primitive church to our fellow Christians. Perhaps that might carry a little more weight than the dismissive "after the apostles were all martyred, the priesthood was taken from the Earth." If our investigators were to be given a way to see that even the early church leaders acknowledged that the church was slowly starting to disintegrate from within, they might look more favorably on the possibility of an apostasy.

I read a book once whose title I cannot remember. At one point the author said something like, "I should stop this book here, but I'm going to go on." He was right. After that point, the book got really weird. Likewise, I should stop this chapter here. But there is more that needs to be said. And it is going to be weird.

Ready?

I personally do not think the priesthood ever completely disappeared. I think what happened was something like what happened with the so-called "fall of Rome."

Historians like to say that the Roman Empire ended in 476 CE when Odoacer, the Germanic potentate, took the throne and royal regalia from Romulus Augustulus. But something like this had happened plenty of times before, as when Maximinus Thrax killed Alexander or when Diocletian usurped the throne from Numerian and Carinus. Dynasties had already come and gone. It is true that this time around, the new ruler did not speak the same language as his predecessor. But Romanism did not begin and end with the nationality or language of the emperor; its system was deeply ingrained in the myriad of nationalities that had become amalgamated into the Roman Empire over the past four or five centuries. But, yes, the central government did change and weaken over time, and thus Romanism began shifting in its various regions.

Consider, for example, what happened to the official Roman

---

14. Eusebius, *Church History*, 3.32.8.

language, Latin. In the Italian peninsula, dialects of Latin evolved into mostly mutually comprehensible Italian. Across the Alps to the north, where the Gauls had become thoroughly Romanized, the gradual linguistic successor was French. And beyond the Pyrenees another deeply ingrained Roman culture let its Latin slowly drift into Spanish. The languages are not far distant. Spaniards and Italians, if they listen closely enough, can converse, each in their own language. Had it been left up to these inheritors of the mother tongue, Latin itself would have completely died out. As it was, the Britannians, whose primary language was never displaced by the Roman language, kept their Latin pristine and correct, and it was the influence of the Irish and English who, a few hundred years later, brought about a restoration of Latin in Europe. Indeed, the Italians, the French, and the Spanish did not realize that they no longer spoke pure Latin.

So the Roman Empire never really fell; rather, its administration gradually devolved to various regional governors, among the strongest of who were Christian bishops. Meanwhile grain ships kept arriving from Egypt, coins continued to be minted, the aqueducts and sewers continued to be kept in trim, and farmers still came to market crossroads to sell their wares.

I posit that, in the same way, the priesthood was never revoked, allowed to die, or taken away. It may have started out as a pure "Latin" with a strong central government, but now it lives on in variegated fashion among the priests, pastors, and parishioners of many a Christian denomination today.

But do they have the *priesthood*? Again, I want to argue yes. After a fashion.

In the Church of Jesus Christ of Latter-day Saints we believe in two orders of the priesthood: one after the order of the Son of God (Melchizedek) and one after the order of Levi (Aaronic). The former presides over the latter and exercises keys that direct the ordinances of exaltation while the latter performs the ordinances of salvation.

According to latter-day revelations, Moses exercised the keys of the higher priesthood to delegate the leadership of the lesser priesthood to Aaron and his progeny, and the D&C states that the Levitical priesthood can be passed down from father to son, and that should any literal descendant of Aaron be found, he has a legal right to it (D&C 68:15–16). So, though the keys of the higher priesthood were lost somewhere between Peter and Joseph Smith, the Aaronic Priesthood is still present and inheritable.

This passing down of priesthood need not necessarily be accomplished by righteousness people or orderly procedure. In the LP&S, where we read of Samuel's succession to the high priesthood of Eli (1 Sam. 3:15–21), we also read that Eli's own two sons, Hophni and Phinehas, were absolute reprobates (1 Sam. 2:12–17), which makes us surmise that Eli himself might not have been the very best of men seeing as how he let his sons extort the meat of offerings and cavort with women serving at the temple. But Samuel's priesthood authority was undiminished by the taintedness of the hands that ordained him. Apparently, priesthood authority can be transmitted by those who have that authority in name but exercise no real priesthood power. In the Book of Mormon, Alma the Elder was ordained a priest under King Noah's direction—certainly not the best man in history (Mosiah 11:5)—yet Alma went on to establish the Nephite church and baptize hundreds, apparently without any other hands being laid upon his head (Mosiah 25:19). Even in LDS Church history, we have documented occurrences of less-than-desirable men passing priesthood authority to people who go on to wield it with godly power. So, despite some horrendous men having held the office of pope, could it not be that there is some dribble of authority that has survived the centuries, even being passed on to Protestant clergy along the way?

I think there is, and I think Latter-day Saints even recognize their priesthood. Here is how: The only people who have to pay the price for their sins are those who in the afterlife go to the Telestial Kingdom (D&C 76:102–6). But the "honorable men of the earth, who were blinded by the craftiness of men" are heirs to the Terrestrial Kingdom, and thus to the forgiveness of their sins (vv. 71–79). Jesus reigns over the Terrestrial Kingdom, and he said that only those who are baptized can come into his kingdom. Every Christian denomination baptizes their members. So can we not say that Christian preachers, priests, and pastors have a certain priesthood that authorizes them to perform the kind of baptism that qualifies their faithful for entry into the Terrestrial Kingdom? We say that Christian denominations are teaching a gospel that contains less than a fullness, but are their efforts still not the work of the Lord? Do you not think that in some way he orders and authorizes those who officiate in this work?

I think we Latter-day Saints are wrong when we declare that other denominations have no authority, that their baptisms are worthless, and that they do not have the gospel. The Lord has said where two or three gather in his name, there he will be also (Matt. 18:20). In our zeal to preach a baptism that opens the way to a higher kingdom, we miss the fact that what they already have is very much a heritage from the Lord. The beliefs and baptisms of these denominations qualify their adherents for salvation in the Terrestrial kingdom where they will enjoy fellowship with the Son: "These are they who receive of the presence of the Son, but not of the fulness of the Father." (D&C 76:77) Their baptism is not worthless; it brings them to Jesus. Is this not worthy in and of itself? Perhaps if we would remember that our baptism qualifies one for fellowship with the Father in the Celestial kingdom, then we could both acknowledge the worth of their baptism while still holding inviolate the surpassing quality of our own.

I now climb off my shaky tree limb and wrap this chapter up. While we do not know when the keys of the Melchizedek Priesthood failed to be transmitted to a rightful and authorized person, we do know, according to revelation, that Peter, James, and John returned to pass them on to Joseph Smith. But just because those keys were lost does not mean that God's power to order his church was immediately lost at the death of the Twelve, nor even quickly diluted during the years immediately following. It may well be that the supervisors of Rome, as well as Antioch, Jerusalem, Alexandria, and what would become other great bishoprics and patriarchates, exercised legitimate power and authority for many years to come.

# PETER WAS THE LAST PERSON TO HOLD PRIESTHOOD KEYS

The dominant LDS view about the Melchizedek Priesthood is that since the post-mortal Peter, James, and John passed its keys to Joseph Smith and Oliver Cowdery, they must have been the last ones to hold those keys. But I think there is a lot of evidence against this view. Even though, yes, the man whom I consider as my prophet, Spencer W. Kimball, said such things as, "In due time [Joseph Smith] received [priesthood] authority under the hands of those who last held the keys upon the earth."[1] And "In quick succession there came other visitors. Peter, James, and John—men who last held the keys of the kingdom, the power of the priesthood, and the blessings of eternity—appeared to [Joseph Smith]."[2]

It is a tall order. So I am going to start with the scriptures, then head into scholarship.

I begin with Jesus' prophecy to Peter that the gates of hell will not prevail against the church (Matt. 16:18), and I take him at his word. It seems a stretch to decide that Jesus then structured his church so that the keys of the priesthood would be lost as soon as the original Twelve Apostles were dead. Was Jesus not the Son of God, the Great Jehovah who participated in every step of the Plan of Happiness? Was he not the greatest prophet of all? Then why would he prophesy that no force could prevail against the church and only a couple decades later instruct his apostles to give up on the priesthood he had given them?

In our LDS efforts to stand apart from the Roman Church and all

---

1. Spencer W. Kimball, "We Thank Thee O God for a Prophet," *Ensign*, Jan. 1973.
2. Spencer W. Kimball, "The Stone Cut without Hands," *Ensign*, May 1976.

its descendants, we tend to look back at the first problems the primitive church encountered and decide that anything resembling true religion just disappeared at that point. We feel we must reject anything that is not the pure church we imagine Christ's original apostles led.

Presumably, Jesus knew the instant he walked away from continual communion with the Twelve that lumps, warts, and unseemly blemishes would start to sprout up. John Welch wrote a fascinating article in *Early Christians in Disarray* that analyzes the JST Bible version of the parable of the sower, comparing it to its counterpart in D&C 86.[3] He argues that Jesus acknowledged the corruption of the church would be a gradual process, not a sudden invasion of locusts. Jesus talks of tares or weeds sprouting up in an otherwise wonderful field of grain. But do a few stray weeds a useless field make? Does a wart destroy beauty? Does long hair invalidate a priesthood ordinance?

I believe that Jesus knew what was coming and did everything in his power to set up a priesthood organization that would have the best chance of succeeding for as long as possible. He was obviously capable of doing so. Remember that in the Book of Mormon the Bountiful church, under the direction of the Twelve Disciples in the Americas, succeeded for 250 years before it began to fall into disrepair. The Three Nephites surely did not single-handedly administer the church after the original disciples departed on their seventy-second birthdays. Certainly, they appointed successors to those vacancies (4 Ne. 14) as the church spread over the whole land (4 Ne. 17). We are happy to acknowledge the existence of this church without worrying about our own claims to restoration, perhaps because it seems that the Mayans, Aztecs, and Spaniards so thoroughly obliterated any trace of that church. Why do we allow the continuance of the Bountiful church but doom the Jerusalem church to an immediate apostasy?

There is even more evidence for the continuance of priesthood keys from patristic and apocryphal literature usually unknown to Latter-day Saints. Based on the *Liber Pontificalis*, a man named Clement was possibly mentioned by Paul as being one who had struggled with him in the ministry, and whose name is "in the book

---

3. Welch, "Modern Revelation," 101–32.

of life" (Philip. 4:3). Although the Roman Church lists Clement as the third in succession to Peter (as pointed out in chapter two), in the eyes of a Latter-day Saint reader, it looks more as if the men listed first and second in succession were actually administrators co-ordinate with Peter, while Clement is the successor to the leader of the primitive church. In any case, in one of his letters, Clement reports to James that Peter said:

> ["]The day of my death is approaching, I lay hands upon this Clement as your bishop. ... Wherefore I communicate to him the power of binding and loosing, so that with respect to everything which he shall ordain in the earth, it shall be decreed in the heavens. For he shall bind what ought to be bound, and loose what ought to be loosed, as knowing the role of the church.["] ... Having thus spoken, he laid his hands upon me in the presence of all, and compelled me to sit in his own chair.[4]

So we have the senior apostle in a conference of priesthood brethren announcing his successor, sitting him down in a chair, lay-ing hands on his head, and ordaining him as supervisor with the power of binding and loosing on heaven and earth. This description fits well with how we LDS Restorationists describe a new apostle or president being set apart. Later in the same record, Peter instructs Clement to send a summary of these events to James in Jerusalem.

> I entreat you, in the presence of all the brethren here, that whensoever I depart from this life, as depart I must, you send to James the brother of the Lord a brief account of your reasonings from your boyhood, and how from the beginning until now you have journeyed with me, hearing the discourse preached by me in every city, and seeing my deeds. And then at the end you will not fail to inform him of the manner of my death, as I said before. For that event will not grieve him very much, when he knows that I piously went through what it behooved me to suffer. And he will get the greatest comfort when he learns that not an unlearned man, or one ignorant of life-giving words, or not knowing the rule of the Church, shall be entrusted with the chair of the teacher after me.[5]

Why did Peter instruct Clement to send a report to James? The James in question is not the James of Peter, James, and John. That

---

4. Anonymous, *Epistle of Clement to James*, 7, 15.
5. Anonymous, *Epistle of Clement to James*, 15–16.

James was killed by Herod in 42 CE. Nor is he the man who succeeded him in the supervision of the Jerusalem branch, presumably
Jesus' cousin James of Alphaeus. That man died in about 62 CE,
several years before this event should have taken place. Could this
James, referred to as "the Brother of the Lord," be Jesus' equivalent
of Joseph Smith's brother Hyrum?

What follows is 100 percent conjecture on my part, but you
might find it plausible. When a vacancy opened in the First Presidency after 42 CE, the apostles wanted to ordain someone who had
"companied with us all the time that the Lord Jesus went in and
out among us" (Acts 1:21). Who better to fill that slot than Jesus'
faithful brother James? It is possible as well that James, either by
Peter selecting him from the Twelve or by advancement as some
other apostle died, was chosen to fill one of the vacancies in the First
Presidency. This would help make sense why, of all people, Peter instructed Clement to announce his elevation to the president of the
First Quorum to James who was serving as counselor along with
John. The Epistle of Clement basically has James being announced,
sustained, and ordained to the office during what Latter-day Saints
call a regional conference of the church in Rome. His epistle was
meant to spark the announcement and sustaining of Clement in a
yet-to-be-held regional conference in Jerusalem.

You may still be struggling with some things that do not sound
right to the LDS ear. For example, Peter appears here to set Clement
apart without the unanimous consent of the Twelve. But, as pointed
out previously, the original Twelve might have been organized differently from the modern Twelve. The apostles served in areas so
distant that communicating with each other, much less getting together for a meeting, was next to impossible. We have no record of
any meeting of the Twelve after 49–50 CE, even though Peter lived
at least another fifteen years. It may be that each of them was set
apart with the right to pass on his own priesthood keys.

That part is not my own conjecture. It was established by Clement of Rome that the apostles gave instructions that other approved
men should succeed to the ministry upon the death of the current
office holders. This injunction comes from 1 Clement, a source
that, although not included in the canon of the GE&A, is widely

recognized by patristic authors, modern scholars, and LDS historians as completely authentic.

> Our apostles also knew, through our Lord Jesus Christ, that there would be strife on account of the office of the episcopate. For this reason, therefore, inasmuch as they had obtained a perfect foreknowledge of this, they appointed those [ministers] already mentioned, and afterwards gave instructions, that when these should fall asleep, other approved men should succeed them in their ministry. We are of opinion, therefore, that those appointed by them, or afterwards by other eminent men, with the consent of the whole church, and who have blamelessly served the flock of Christ, in a humble, peaceable, and disinterested spirit, and have for a long time possessed the good opinion of all, cannot be justly dismissed from the ministry.[6]

Just because modern apostles enact everything as a unanimous body—setting the next president apart with the entire quorum—does not mean that that was the way it was done 2,000 years ago. Consider the changes to modern priesthood policy and practice: the discontinuance of the priesthood office of seventy, the modification to the office of high priest, and the adjustment in advancement ages of Aaronic Priesthood holders (allowing eleven-year-old deacons). We believe the Lord directs the adaptation of the organization of the priesthood to match the needs of the current generation. Are we justified in thinking that the way the modern Quorum of Twelve is organized is any indication of how the original Twelve was set up?

Did Clement pass the keys on to his successor? The *Liber Pontificalis* says that he was supervisor from 69 to 79 CE, during which time he apparently presided over a large boundary reorganization which ended up dividing the church (whether in Rome or worldwide is unknown) into seven districts. However, it states that he didn't die until Trajan had become emperor, which took place at least twenty years after the stated beginning of his supervision of the church. His death also allegedly took place near Sevastopol, Ukraine, where he had been sent as a political prisoner. Were he to get a shield, like the apostles in chapter one, it would feature an anchor, as he is reputed to have been tied to one and cast into the

---

6. Clement of Rome, *Epistle to the Corinthians*, 242.

Black Sea. There is no record anywhere, however, of the supervisory position in Rome experiencing any protracted or difficult vacancy. So, while we cannot hope to establish with any hint of accuracy when the keys were no longer transmitted, we can at least be confident that Peter was not their last possessor and that Clement likely passed them on as well.

A quick side note here regarding the *Liber Pontificalis*. The book claims to be a chronicle of the Catholic popes from the very beginning. It seems Jerome played the part of Mormon in gathering various sources into a single document in the mid fourth century CE. Beyond that, items were added by various authors over the next four centuries. The book has been heavily edited and redacted, thus calling into question the historical accuracy of any or all of it. However, I cite these few excerpts with confidence because of the following rationale. The fact that their description is so like to that that a modern Saint would recognize as the transfer of keys shows that it is improbable that the Catholic church would have counterfeited the account. It would be far more indicative of forgery if it were more like any of the subsequent historical papal transfers. Also, acknowledging that even Eusebius in 325 CE did not understand the concurrency of Linus' and Cletus' overseership with Peter marks them not as good he first two papal successors, but perhaps more as what we Saints would associate with assistants to the Twelve or stake presidents, shows that this document from very early on was misunderstood by ecclesiastical authorities, and therefore unlikely to be forged or doctored.

I now point out something that you may not have noticed while reading through to this point. Whenever I have referred to the original Twelve, I have never used the word *quorum*. That is because using such a term would be anachronistic. The word never occurs anywhere in the LP&S and GE&A or in the BoM, though it does appear six times in the D&C. Our Twelve function as a quorum because that is how the Lord revealed it to Joseph Smith. That does not necessarily mean the Lord set up the leadership of his church in Jerusalem or Bountiful the same way.

I have belabored this point to create, I hope, sufficient room for the possibility that the original apostles were authorized to appoint their own successors and to endow them with the necessary keys to function in their offices. Not only is there no documentation stating that they had to meet as a quorum to make changes, but there *is* documentation and tradition from primitive and post-primitive church records that priesthood keys indeed continued.

The original twelve apostles did not all die suddenly as martyrs. The apostolic priesthood did not suddenly cease when they were gone. Rather, it lived on in its designated successors. Those successors organized, with power and authority, an ever-widening community of believers. Even the sealing and presiding power was passed on for at least one generation. And even after those keys eventually ceased to be passed down, there were still righteous men and women exercising their legitimate priesthood authority in power to guide the faithful for many years.

All right, I have made my argument, but perhaps some of the scholarly among you have been waving your hands in the air for a while now. You want to point out that some of the apocryphal sources I have cited are not necessarily accepted as authentic by scholars. I would like to think of myself as a scholar too, and I tend to put great weight upon what other scholars write. However, one area where I am not yet convinced of scholarly opinion is their questioning of the authenticity of both canonical and apocryphal writings.

For example, some scholars contend that Paul's epistles to Timothy and Titus (called the Pastoral Epistles because they address concerns of pastors, or those who have authority over church communities) are pseudonymous—that they were written by someone else who signed Paul's name to the letters to give them the impression of authenticity. However, they do this in the face of considerable patristic acceptance of these epistles as genuine. They were included in, cited by, or quoted by the following: Jerome, Polycarp, Irenaeus, Clement of Alexandria, Tertullian, Origen, Eusebius, Athanasius of Alexandria—as well as being included in early versions of the GE&A: Peshitta, Muratorian Canon, Codex Sinaiticus, and Latin Vulgate.[7] Even Eusebius does not express any reservations about the

---

7. Metzger, *The Canon of the New Testament,* 197.

Pastorals. Of all the patristic writers, only Marcion and Tatian expressed any hesitation about one or more of the epistles.

Some scholars also contend that because these epistles contain emergent Catholicism (the church hierarchy of bishops, priests, etc.), they are most probably pseudonymous.[8] They think it is impossible that any sort of church leadership could have emerged within Paul's lifetime.[9] Such scholars suppose that neither Peter nor Paul could respond to changes in the community of developing orthodoxy with any effectiveness.

I think this is a pretty dim opinion of both men, casting Peter as an illiterate who could speak only Aramaic, and Paul, despite his brilliant mind, as incapable of learning in his later years. As for Peter's lack of linguistic ability, we should remember that his brother's name was Andrew, or *Andros*, a Greek name, showing that Peter's parents at least had knowledge of and sympathy for the Greek language and culture (Matt. 4:18). As for being just a fisherman, we should remember that Peter was able to run a business whose operation he could largely vacate for several years before returning to immediately take up again (John 21:3). In other words, scholars have dismissed the dynamism that accompanies the type of men we Latter-day Saints see filling the ranks of the Twelve as they rise to intellectual and spiritual excellence under the influence of the Holy Ghost. We can certainly detect a dramatic change in Peter's personality only a month or two after the crucifixion. What could he become with an additional thirty years? As for Paul, he might have brought more preexisting theological baggage with him on the road to Damascus than Peter brought from Galilee, but unlike Athena springing fully formed and battle-ready from Zeus' head, his ideas were not set in stone. Just like Brother Joseph over an even shorter time, I believe Peter and Paul were capable of accepting and proposing new directions for communal organization that would make it possible to establish a priesthood structure that could survive them.[10]

---

8. Perrin, Duling, and Ferm, *The New Testament*, 265.

9. Ehrman, *The New Testament*, 391.

10. A second reason scholars dismiss Paul's Pastoral Epistles as pseudepigraphal is because the vocabulary has been reported to be markedly different from his other correspondence in the canon. One scholar, writing in a time when character-based computer

Earlier in this chapter, I quoted from a relatively undisputed epistle of Clement to the saints at Corinth, often referred to as 1 Clement. The pseudo-Clementine writings, sometimes referred to as 2 Clement, contain the *Homilies*, the *Recognitions*, and two letters— one from Peter and one from Clement, both addressed to James at Jerusalem. Scholars who have examined the *Homilies* and *Recognitions*, comparing them both textually and doctrinally to other patristic writings, date them to anywhere from the second to the fourth centuries CE.[11] So they are unlikely to be authentic. But I did not quote from them. I did, however, quote from the letters because I have yet to find any substantive scholarly analysis of them, and my own analysis makes me think they are authentic. Here's why.

The letter has Peter writing to James, the head of the primitive church in Jerusalem:

> I beg and beseech you not to communicate to any one of the gentiles the books of my preaching which I sent to you, nor to any one of our own tribe *before trial*; but if anyone has been proved and found worthy, then to commit them to him. ... Give the books of my preaching to our brethren, with the like *mystery of initiation*, that they may indoctrinate

---

analysis of text was unavailable, reports that the Pastoral Epistles consist of 848 words (not including proper names), 306 of which do not occur in any other of the Pauline epistles that are considered authentic. Thus, over 36 percent of the Pastorals' vocabulary is unique, throwing their authenticity into doubt (Harrison, *The Problem of the Pastoral Epistles,* 21). However, my own character-based computer analysis of these numbers results in 956 distinct words in the Pastorals, 573 of which do not occur in any other Pauline epistle. This brings Paul's overall vocabulary to 5,671 words, of which the distinct 573 words in the Pastorals come to about 10 percent, less than one third of the earlier scholar's estimate. (These numbers were arrived at by downloading the Greek text for each Pauline epistle from greekbible.com, collating these words into a document from which all duplicates were removed, and then loading the results into a relational database, from which queries were run to find all words that exist in the Pastoral epistles that are not otherwise present in the authentic or deutero-Pauline epistles. Proper names and numeric words were also removed.) Ten percent may appear substantial at first glance, but let us compare it to Brother Joseph's canonical writings. In the first dozen years, his vocabulary comes to 2,864 words. But during the last several years of his writings, which contain his more literary compositions, his vocabulary falls to 2,167 words, 831 of which were not used in the first dozen years: 38 percent. The same approach was used here as was used in the Pauline text analysis. The revelations from 1820 to 1832 comprise the first dataset, while those from 1838 to 1844 comprise the second dataset.) Clearly the evolution of an author's published vocabulary from one period of life to another is not indicative of a change in authorship.

11. Jones and Duncan, "Pseudo-Clementines."

those who wish to take part in teaching; for if it be not so done, our word of truth will be rent into many opinions.[12]

Peter had apparently previously sent James some sort of correspondence that contained teachings that were not for general consumption. The trial he mentions is later explained as an initiatory ordinance that taught the hidden doctrines of Peter to disciples of six years tenure. During the ordinance, they made covenants not to reveal the teachings to anyone on pain of death. When I suggest that "the mysteries of the Kingdom" may be what comprise the LDS temple ordinance, and note that prior to 1991 endowment participants covenanted to keep certain parts of the ceremony sacred on pain of symbolic death, I speculate that Peter is giving directions about how (and to whom) to administer his dispensation's version of the endowment. Because of its content, Latter-day Saints may judge the Clementine letter of Peter to James as both genuine and revealing. It is also additional evidence, I believe, that the apostles were not engaged in closing up shop in the face of an approaching apostasy; they were, after all, waiting at least six years to endow new disciples. Clearly they were planning for the long haul.

One last point about who held the keys of the priesthood during early Christian history. The D&C and Joseph Smith's teachings say that the keys of the priesthood and the keys to a *dispensation of the priesthood* are not one and the same. Latter-day Saints sing with gusto of Joseph Smith, "ever and ever the keys he will hold," even though we believe the current president holds and exercises all priesthood keys. Joseph ordained the Twelve with all priesthood keys, and yet he retains the keys to the Dispensation of the Fullness of Times. Was it not possible then that Peter, despite permanently holding the keys of the Dispensation of the Meridian of Time, passed on all priesthood keys to a mortal successor in his own time? This entire chapter argues that he did.

---

12. Anonymous, *Epistle of Peter to James*, 1–2.

## MYTH 5

# THE CHURCH BROKE UP INTO MANY PIECES

When I was a nineteen-year-old LDS missionary, I somehow inherited a mental picture of a mirror that represented the primitive Christian church. The mirror lost its moorings to the wall (the priesthood) and fell to the ground, shattering into hundreds of shards. Each shard contained a small fragment of the gospel of Jesus Christ. That was the great apostasy. I do not know where I got that image; perhaps it was something passed on to me by my senior companion. Sometimes I wondered why it had to be a mirror. Why not a ripped-up book or a shattered pot? In any case, I found out that I am not the only one carrying this image in my head. While researching this topic, I came across several LDS web pages using the same metaphor. One was a blog post where the author said he was planning on shattering a mirror as part of a talk he was giving on the apostasy and restoration at a youth conference. Another was an idea for a Primary lesson complete with less dangerous graphics of a broken mirror.[1] The metaphor is apparently a popular one. But is it anywhere near correct?

I bet you can guess my answer. But before I dive into my reasoning, I want to let you know that when I discuss various Christian churches, I refer to them as denominations. Once, when my wife and I were touring a distant city, we attended a worship service in a famous chapel. Afterward, I had a few questions to ask the man who led the service. I prefaced my first question by saying, "I am not of your faith," but he immediately, though gently, corrected me. "We are all of the same faith," he said. "You are simply of another

---

1. Mary Ross et al., "APOSTASY - Restoration: LDS Lesson Activity - Apostasy Mirror Teaching Tool, 'Why Was the Restoration Necessary?' Stand as a Witness," *Gospel Grab Bag*, Jan. 10, 2013.

denomination." I felt not only his kindly rebuke, but a spiritual confirmation of its truth. So I use denomination to remind us that we are of the same faith as the various "shards" we talk about.

How many modern Christian denominations are there? You might begin by counting Catholic, Lutheran, Episcopalian, Baptist, Methodist, Presbyterian, and Jehovah's Witnesses, and think you are getting close. In truth you have only started the car and backed down the driveway. Grandma's house is still a long way away. Want to know how far? Take a moment to look up "List of Christian denominations" on Wikipedia, for example.[2] No, I am not going to give you the total. I want you to experience the never-ending variety of that list, and the names and locations of Christian denominations you never even considered.

But, of course, that is a list that has had 2,000 years to develop. The question we would like to answer here is, "How many *post-primitive* denominations were there?" Sadly, that number is ultimately unknowable since records describing that time are so scarce. Instead, let us talk about how these schisms erupted.

Usually, an influential person would accentuate a single point of doctrine as a differentiating factor between his views and someone else's. At first, it was the peculiarity of the doctrine that made its adherents pride themselves on being one step ahead of their brethren, but eventually the movement would coalesce around the main emphasizer of that peculiar doctrine. This is why many of the early schisms, later called heresies, are named after people: Marcion's or Donatus' or Montanus' heresy. But the reason these were called heresies was because there was still a main body of believers that remained true to Jesus' original teachings. So factions did break off, and they were noisy and noticeable, but this does not mean that everyone went simultaneously astray as the shattered mirror metaphor might lead you to believe.

The following is a survey of some of these groups. We call them the Ebionites, the Marcionites, the Montanists, the Arians, the Sabellians, and the Gnostics. Any historians who might be reading, please note

---

2. "List of Christian Denominations," *Wikipedia*.

that I talk about the veracity of the sources I use to describe these groups after I finish explaining what those sources tell us.

First, let us turn to the *Ebionites*. Sources hint that they were a group of saints centered on James (Jesus' brother) in Jerusalem who were warned to escape the city before the Romans besieged and destroyed it in 70 CE. The group ended up in a town called Pella, now known as Tabaqat Fahl on the Jordanian side of the Jordan River about an hour's drive south of the Sea of Galilee.[3] However, it is not clear how large this group was. Some scholars limit the number of converts to the early church to around 1,000 persons, most of whom lived in Jerusalem.[4] However, Jesus did the lion's share of his preaching around Galilee, with only annual visits to Jerusalem, so there were probably plenty of converts in the communities surrounding Jerusalem as well.

It is not known if the group's name derives from the founder's name, Ebion, or from the ancient Hebrew אביון, a word meaning *poor*.[5] We do not know if group members used the name themselves. One scholar classifies them as "Jewish-Christian Adoptionists." The Jewish-Christian part means that they were Jews who had accepted Jesus as the Messiah and insisted that in order to become a Christian you first had to become a Jew.[6] The adoptionist part means that they believed that prior to his baptism Jesus was fully a mortal man— so the literal son of Joseph through Mary. Only after his baptism, when God the Father (according to Psalms) said "this day have I begotten thee," did Jesus become divine.[7] These saints had such distaste for Paul and his epistles that they totally ignored them. There is even conjecture that they centered their doctrine on a version of the Gospel of Matthew that said that ακρίδα [akrisa], the word for locust, was actually supposed to be ἐγκρίς [egkris], a word meaning honey-cake. Thus they believed that John the Baptist was not an eater of locusts, but a vegetarian; and so were they. This is not a doctrinal difference that would have separated them denominationally, but rather a cultural difference that they allowed to drive a wedge

---

3. Eusebius, *Church History*, 3.5.3.

4. Stark, *Cities of God*, 67.

5. Origen, *On First Principles*, 4.22.

6. Justin Martyr, *Dialogue with Trypho*, 47.

7. Tertullian, *On the Flesh of Christ*, 14, 18, 24.

between them and their fellow believers. Such teachings, however, led later church fathers such as Tertullian and Epiphanius to label them as "heresies." Even with their vegetarian emphasis, it is ironic that the church fathers labeled the Ebionites as "heretics" since their doctrines were closer to what Jesus' apostles taught than what would later be adopted in the Nicaean Creed.[8]

But here we see the beginnings of schism in the church, to which Paul referred when he scolded the Corinthians for claiming that they were with Paul, Apollos, Cephas (Peter), or Jesus (1 Cor. 1:12). Indeed, one other myth I briefly address here is that the primitive church was a monolithic, hierarchical institution like the our present LDS Church. More likely, it was a somewhat disjointed movement made up of loosely connected communities who themselves were often in strong disagreement. The primitive Christian church, even with the apostles alive and well, suffered a severe *cultural* rift from the very beginning.

One of the main rifts was between the Petrines and the Paulines. The Ebionites, being Jewish-Christians (also called Judaizers), were those who, with Peter, believed that converts to Christianity still had to follow the Law of Moses. Thus they were called Petrines. Those who sided with Paul were the Paulines.

We have at least two instances of Paul and Peter clashing over this dichotomy. The first was at the church conference in Jerusalem in about 50 CE, where Peter promulgated the following compromise: "Therefore I conclude that we should not cause extra difficulty for those among the gentiles who are turning to God, but that we should write them a letter telling them to abstain from things defiled by idols and from sexual immorality and from what has been strangled and from blood" (Acts 15:19–20).

Later, during a visit to Antioch, Peter was apparently having dinner with the gentile converts when some Jewish-Christian saints arrived from Jerusalem. Peter sneaked away from dinner, afraid they would see him fraternizing with the gentile converts. Paul, noticing how congregations had begun following Peter's example by separating themselves between Jewish-Christians and gentile-Christians,

---

8. Ehrman, "Christians Who Would Be Jews."

blew up at Peter, saying, "If you, although you are a Jew, live like a gentile and not like a Jew, how can you try to force the gentiles to live like Jews?" (Gal. 2:11–14).

Hence, the first great schism, even before the demise of the apostles, was between the Petrines and the Paulines. However, both sides agreed on the same gospel principles and the authority of the apostles. Their disagreements ran basically along cultural lines. Perhaps we could compare it to one of the great cultural divides in the LDS Church: those Petrine saints who abstain from cola because of its caffeine content, and those Pauline members who indulge in "many liters of a diet soda that shall remain nameless."[9] There are even more dramatic schisms to come.

There appears to be another rift between apostles, but one that did not become known until the discovery of the Gospel of Thomas, a deuterocanonical collection of the sayings of Jesus composed sometime between 60 and 250 CE, but not brought to light until 1945 when the Nag Hammadi library was unearthed. Only when reading this document in the twentieth century does the rift become visible at all. We do know that John tells the story of the "doubting Thomas" in his gospel, showing that from the beginning Thomas had some misgivings about a physical resurrection, something that probably marks him as having come from a Sadducean background. But only when we compare John's style with the writings in the Gospel of Thomas does this Sadducean interpolation into Christianity show a rift between the two.[10] Another scholar notes that while John requires a strict belief in Jesus' singular ability to save, Thomas also allows for the effectiveness of one's own divinely given capacity.[11] At a distance of two millennia such an argument seems improbable in light of our understanding of the reality of the resurrection. However, when one regards much more recent events of the disagreement between Bruce R. McConkie's "true fellowship all Saints should have with the Father" and BYU professors' establishment of "a personal relationship with Jesus Christ," one can more clearly imagine such a rift in the infancy of Christianity.[12]

---

9. Dieter F. Uchtdorf, "Oh How Great the Plan of Our God!" *Ensign*, Nov. 2016.

10. Gregory J. Riley, *Resurrection Reconsidered: Thomas and John in Controversy*, 177.

11. Elain Pagels, *Beyond Belief*, 34.

12. Bruce R. McConkie, "Our Relationship with the Lord." BYU Speeches, Mar. 1982.

In the second century CE, we hear of a group of saints who are known as *Montanists*. They followed a man named Montanus who lived in the middle of modern Turkey. Montanus was a Pauline who said he was a prophet and had received a "new revelation" which came upon him in ecstatic fits of speaking in tongues in the name of God. Later writers ascribe several separating doctrines to the Montanists, including a belief in a physical resurrection, a willingness to give the priesthood to women, strict laws concerning divorce, and celebrating Easter on a fixed date (14 Nisan) instead of trying to calculate it anew each year. The Montanists were also among the first who thought that suffering martyrdom was a fast pass to heaven. It is worth noting that the famous Tertullian, who wrote volumes against what he regarded as heresies, is purported to have become a believer in the Montanist doctrines later in life.[13]

We also hear of the much-maligned *Gnostics*, or those who believed one was exalted by obtaining mystic knowledge. (By that definition, Mormons are Gnostics, by the way.) We know more about Gnosticism partially because of Irenaeus' long excoriation, *Against Heresies*, and because of a few extra-Biblical fragments, such as the *Gospel of Thomas*. They present an especially complex polytheistic pantheon (like in Greek mythology or Tolkien's *Ainulindalë*), in which the figure of Christ is an unforeseen and accidental addition to the story of the cosmos. However, if you wanted to learn more about Gnostic doctrines, there was not a church or synagogue you could go to. It was not a religion. Neither was it a sect. If you got five Gnostics in a room, they would have at least five different opinions on any religious subject.[14] It was just a set of alternate doctrines that were bandied about in post-primitive LDS Gospel Doctrine classes when the bishopric was not there. Gradually those who became dissatisfied with the plain and precious parts of the Gospel Doctrine class decided it was more fun to haunt the halls during Sunday school ... or simply stay home.

One Gnostic was named Marcion. He was a bishop's kid who tried mixing his philosophies of men (Gnosticism) with scripture (Paul's epistles). His followers were called *Marcionites*. He differed

---

13. Nicola Denzey, "What Did the Montanists Read?," 429.
14. Lapham, *An Introduction to the New Testament Apocrypha*, 186.

from Gnostics in that he believed salvation was not based on secret knowledge but on scripture. But in order for scripture to not contradict his ideas, he had to completely ditch the LP&S, using only one highly edited version of Luke and ten of Paul's epistles.

It was not until the third and fourth centuries CE that actual denominations (instead of heresies or schisms) started to appear. The issue that birthed them was Christology, or the nature of Christ. Was he God? Was he a man? Both? To what degree? There were five main interpretations of this vexing question. *Adoptionism* (as we discussed with the Ebionites) claimed that Jesus was a regular man who, by his righteousness, was adopted by the Father when God pronounced his approval at his baptism. This is based on Paul's speech to the Antiochenes: "You are my son. This very day have I become your father" (Acts 13:33; Ps. 2:7). *Arianism* followed the reasoning of a priest in Alexandria named Arian who preached that there was a time when Jesus was not yet God's son, and that Jesus was subordinate to God, not his absolute equal. *Docetism*, also ostensibly named after the doctrine and not the founder, preached that Jesus was merely an apparition, a phantom—that God could not possibly have existed in a body composed of temporal matter. *Sabellianism*, named after Sabellius, taught that the Godhead was one entity with three different faces or modes

Those are the main heresies and early denominations. But before wrapping up this brief survey, it is time for the other shoe to drop. Everything I have said in this chapter about everyone from Ebionites to Sabellians was written not by the people belonging to those movements, but by their detractors. At best, these detractors commented on a few quotations from the denominations' various writings, and they were very probably taken out of context—what has been called "misleading generalizations and unwarranted stereotypes."[15] (Ancient detractors of Gnosticism were motivated not only by theology but politics.[16]) Relying on these hostile accounts may not be as misleading as trying to learn about Joseph Smith from an

---

15. Smith, *No Longer Jews*, 8.
16. Shelton, *Quest for the Historical Apostles*, 45.

anti-Mormon pamphlet; it is more like trying to gain an understanding of Presbyterianism from an LDS Gospel Doctrine class.[17]

Ebionites are accused of having denied the divinity of Christ—at least up until his baptism. Is this actually what they believed, or did they, like some Latter-day Saints, believe that Jesus suspected but did not actually know of his divine parentage until God declared it from the heavens? Those who called Montanism a heresy wrote that its adherents had the audacity to believe that their new prophesy could contradict the gospel as proclaimed by the apostles. But do not the Latter-day Saints recognize that continuing revelation at times supersedes previous doctrine? The ancient church fathers say that those horrible Montanists allowed women to officiate in the priesthood ordinances, but who knows if it was just women praying in their version of general conference? Opponents wrote that the Gnostics believed true salvation came not by faith, but by secret knowledge based on some sketchy creation stories. The secret knowledge of the Latter-day Saints is based on a story that "figurative" regarding the origins of Adam and Eve and consists of teachings without which we cannot advance in the celestial worlds. One church father accuses the Montanists of being radish-eaters, as if that were of any importance whatsoever.[18] Arianism dared to make the Son subordinate to the Father. Yet the LDS temple ordinance clearly shows who gives the orders and who executes them. Clearly, we see that the authors from whom we glean information about these early Christian movements had a bone to pick and should not be taken entirely at face value.

We see from this brief survey that in the first three centuries of the Common Era, the church had not shattered into a million pieces. If we include Petrines, Paulines, Ebionites, Montanists, Marcionites, Adoptionists, Arians, Docetists, Sabellians, and various flavors of Gnostics, we end up with a dozen or so pieces. However, whether a person baptized by a Marcionite priest felt himself akin to or divorced from his Montanist friend in the next village is hard to say. Each of the church fathers railed against the apostate beliefs of one

---

17. When the Nag Hammadi "library" was unearthed in 1945, it contained some fragments of Gnostic literature. What has been discovered there is beyond the scope of this book, because here we are talking about what we have inherited from the past.

18. Hippolytus, *Refutation of All Heresies*, 8.12.

or another of the sects. Even Eusebius, who at least tried to be neutral, merely quoting what others had said, let his prejudice show in his *Martyrs of Palestine*. When he was cataloging some Christians who were executed by the Roman state, he mentioned that "a certain Asclepius, supposed to be a bishop of the sect of Marcion, possessed as he thought with zeal for religion, but not according to knowledge," was burned to death.[19] Eusebius (who perhaps leaned toward Arianism) could not bring himself to acknowledge that Asclepius was a real martyr because he did not toe Eusebius' Christological line.

Although some pretty esoteric doctrines were being dreamed up, not every deviation was necessarily the result of a devilish individual bent on corruption. One LDS man with whom I had a difficult episode in a church capacity was called to serve in a temple presidency a decade later. He may have been just as surprised to see me officiating in the temple as I was to see him presiding. Even though we could each tell a venomous story about the other, we found ourselves worshiping in the same place. That gives me pause when reading the diatribes of the church fathers against their supposed enemies.

Unlike us, our early Christian counterparts did not have their own personal copies of the scriptures, regular visits from church authorities, or church magazines. These saints were trying their best to follow the gospel with whatever personal priesthood power they had come to wield, whatever spiritual direction they were able to receive, whatever ragged papyrus rolls of scripture they kept in the bishop's closet. Mistakes were made. I think we wrong our early Christian heritage when we forget the faith and effort early saints exerted during the first three centuries following Christ when we blithely say, "After the apostles were killed, the church broke up into many pieces." Perhaps we could be generous and admit that the Christian church managed to maintain some kind of shape for all those centuries—much longer than the Nephite church held out. We should give credit where credit is due.

---

19. Eusebius, *The Martyrs of Palestine*, 10.2.

MYTH 6

# Thousands Suffered
# Inevitable Martyrdom

The myth of Christian martyrs, held by Latter-day Saints and other Christians alike, may be summed up by Jean-Léon Gérôme's 1883 painting *The Christian's Last Prayer*. It is the very first image that is displayed when you do a Google image search for "Christian martyr." Before a capacity crowd in the Colosseum, under the looming background of the emperor's palace, a majestic lion surveys his lunch of at least thirty Christians kneeling in prayer as their patriarch stands to offer a plea to the heavens. At the edge of the arena are visible nine victims who have been crucified and soaked in pitch. Those at the left of the picture have already been set alight, and just to the right of the patriarch a torch is being extended from the seats to light another victim, who twists his body in anticipation of the flames. For this piece, Gérôme broke from his habit of painting his subjects in seductive nudity, possibly so that we could concentrate on the piety of the victims and pity them. But in real life the victims of both crucifixion and *damnatio ad bestias* would have met their fates without a shred of clothing.[1] Such scenes of brutal Christian martyrdom have become a popular historical orthodoxy and are embedded deeply in our collective consciousness. Take, for example, Andrew Hyatt's 2018 film *Paul, Apostle of Christ*. Just three minutes into the film, as Jim Caviezel's Luke secretly enters Rome during the Neronian persecution, he pauses in horror as he encounters a burning, crucified corpse hung on the wall. The camera pans to reveal at least five more such victims at intervals as the street fades into perspective. I never got more than three-and-a-half minutes into the movie, the historic

---

1. Shaw, "The Passion of Perpetua," 8.

fact-bending was more horrifying to me than the burning corpses. No such scene ever played out anywhere in Rome or its empire.

Since the 1950s, scholars have been refuting this received tradition, but the learned opinions of scholarship are slow to trickle down into popular consciousness. While I was writing my master's thesis on this topic, I was earning a bit of side cash driving ride-share. When I got a talkative passenger, I would sometimes ask, "In the first three centuries, how many people were executed for being Christian?" Initially, most of my passengers would not put a number to it, but when I persisted, they usually guessed in the tens of thousands. They were inevitably taken aback when I told them that it was fewer than 200. Indeed, Candida Moss's 2014 book on the subject (that has been read by regular people as well as historians) has this to say:

> Christians were not constantly persecuted, hounded, or targeted by the Romans. Very few Christians died, and when they did, they were often executed for what we in the modern world would call political reasons.[2]

What are the actual stories of Christian martyrdom? First, I should note that these stories do not actually start until 300 CE, when, for about a decade, a couple of Roman emperors, for various reasons, made it somewhat illegal to practice Christianity. But in far-away Britannia, the head Roman official decided that he would not enforce the edict, perhaps because his wife was a Christian. A few years later, in 313 CE, his son Constantine managed to claw his way up to the emperor's throne where he issued an edict that Christians were no longer to be singled out and that their property should be restored to them. This was the beginning of a newly recognized Christianity that stood on equal footing with the official Roman religion. Most staunch Romans could live with that. But, when in 381 CE Emperor Theodosius banned all religions except that taught by the Bishop of Rome, it was too much for the traditional Romans. Bad feelings surfaced in various ways until the Christians of the fourth and fifth centuries CE felt compelled to recount just how much they had been persecuted by the pagans, perhaps somewhat like how Latter-day Saints recount the legacy of our murdered prophet and displaced pioneer forebears in order to claim our own martyr badge.

---

2. Moss, *The Myth of Persecution*, 14.

One of these Christians was Sulpicius Severus, a Christian pres-
byter who lived from about 363 to 420 CE in the Roman province
of Aquitania (southwestern France). He wrote a world history from
a churchman's point of view titled *Sacred History*. In the second book
of that work, he outlines nine separate events, which he labeled *per-
secutio*, and assigns to them the names of the emperors who reigned
during the time of the violence.[3] Over the years, several authors
have added or subtracted from that list, but usually they stick to an
even ten—to match the number of plagues in the story of Exodus.[4]
The following is a summary of these supposed persecutions and a
comparison between their traditional lore and the findings of more
modern historians.

## 1. Nero's Persecution (64 CE)

The first persecution is attributed to Nero, the one depicted by the
painting and movie discussed above. The Roman author Tacitus tells
a story of the Great Fire of Rome consuming a huge portion of the
city in the summer of 64 CE. (Tacitus was a young man when the fire
occurred.) We often hear that Nero sat in his palace on the Palatine
Hill playing his fiddle while Rome burned,[5] but, in fact, he was thirty
or forty miles away in his seaside villa in Anzio.[6] He immediately
rushed back to the city and began implementing disaster recovery
protocols, opening public lands for the displaced to lodge upon and
distributing massive amounts of food. However, when he began buy-
ing up the burnt-out properties where he would eventually erect his
*domus aurea*, people smelled a rat. Conspiracy theories began to cir-
culate about shadowy groups of people who kept the fire brigade
from getting to the fires. So Nero pinned the blame on a group of
undesirables, who, after a little torture, identified a larger group of
co-conspirators who were summarily convicted. Since the crime was
arson, Roman law specified death by fire. Nero decided to make the
execution into a bit of theater. Tacitus records that the convicts "were

---

3. Severus, *Sacred History*, 2.31–33.
4. V. Grumel, "Du Nombre des Persécutions Païennes dans les Anciennes Chro-
niques," *Revue d'Etudes Augustiniennes et Patristiques* 2, nos. 1–2 (1956): 61.
5. Gyles, "Nero Fiddled While Rome Burned," 211–17.
6. Tacitus, *Annals*, 15.39.

covered with wild beasts' skins and torn to death by dogs; or they were fastened on crosses, and, when daylight failed were burned to serve as lamps by night" in Nero's gardens.[7] But though the city was pacified regarding the fire, they grew to hate Nero because of his ferocity in punishing the supposed culprits. It is from this account that we inherit our first images of Christian persecutions.

I should start by saying that, yes, some of Nero's victims were likely Christian. Tacitus describes them as *Chrestians*, but it is very likely that he had simply misspelled Christians since he goes on to say that the founder of the group "had undergone the death penalty in the reign of Tiberius, by sentence of the procurator Pontius Pilatus" (though that sentence may have been added by a later scribe). However, they were not being punished *because* they were Christian. We infer this from the fact that no Christian writers portrayed this event as a religious persecution until 300 years later.

Tertullian, who wrote at the turn of the third century CE, speaks only of Peter and Paul being murdered in Rome. Eusebius, who tried to be as exhaustive as humanly possible, mentions the atrocities of Nero, including the killing of Peter and Paul, but makes absolutely no mention of the fire victims.[8] Lactantius, who wrote almost a century later, compares the Great Fire of Rome with the account of the fire that burned down the palace in Nicomedia (an event that indeed sparked the one time that Christianity *did* become illegal). There are too many parallels between Lactantius' and Tacitus' accounts for Lactantius not to have been familiar with his account, and yet Lactantius makes absolutely no mention of Nero's Christian victims.[9] The first mention of the episode by any Christian writer comes up 300 years after the Great Fire in Sulpicius Severus' *Sacred History*.[10] Just a decade or so before Severus, another writer named Orosius had corrected Tacitus' *Chrestians* to *Christians* (along with a possible insertion mentioning Pilate and Christ), or had come into possession of a record already thus interpolated by a previous scribe.[11] It is not hard to conclude, then, that it was Severus, who,

7. Tacitus, *Annals*, 15.44.
8. Eusebius, *Church History*, 2.25.
9. Rougé, "L'incendie de Rome en 64," 441.
10. Severus, *Sacred History*, 2.29.
11. Jobjorn, "Inpulsore Cherestro?," 360.

naively in possession of a record that spoke of some Christian victims, started the tradition that Nero persecuted Christians *because* they were Christian.

## 2. Domitian's Persecution (ca. 95 CE)

There are no hints from the historical record that any other Christians were hindered in any way in any other corner of the Roman Empire until thirty years later during the time of Domitian, Vespasian's second son. There must have been some kind of bad blood between the government and some Christians, for it was at this time that John the apostle was exiled to the island of Patmos where he penned Revelation. But as far as Christian persecution is concerned, only one family is mentioned, the husband being executed, and the wife, like John, being banished.[12] The husband was not punished for being a Christian, however, but for fighting a gladiator. It was suspected that the wife had some fondness for the Jews,[13] but because the wife's name is associated with a plot of land that later became a Christian cemetery, historians have tried to make her into a Christian.[14]

Another incident that bears mentioning, if only to clear it from the record, is Eusebius' note that Domitian had issued a command to kill all descendants of David. He does not mention that any actually were found and killed, or that this would have affected Christians especially. He relates a story where a couple is accused by heretics of being descended from Jesus' brother Judas. When they were brought before Domitian, they showed that their inheritance was only a plot of less than a tenth of a square mile upon which they had worked and paid taxes their whole life. They said that, as Christians, if they were heirs to any kingdom, it was one that would not come until the end of the world. Domitian relented and ceased his search for Davidic heirs.[15] One historian notes that because Domitian is compared to Herod, the tale bears all the marks of a legend, and can be summarily discounted.[16]

---

12. Eusebius, *Church History*, 3.18.5.
13. Dio Cassius, *Historia Romanus*, 67.14.1–2.
14. Hardy, *Christianity and the Roman Government*, 86–88.
15. Eusebius, *Church History*, 3.19–20.
16. Millar, *The Emperor in the Roman World*, 554–55.

## 3. Trajan's Persecution (ca. 105 CE)

In the early second century, a Roman citizen named Pliny, known as "the Younger," was appointed by Emperor Trajan to take over the governorship of a province named Bithynia-Pontus in what is now northwestern Turkey. Pliny kept a copy of all his correspondence with the emperor, and at intervals he packaged it up and sent it to his publishers back in Rome.[17] Hence we have a detailed description of what happened.

The area had been rife with rebellion prior to Pliny's arrival, so Trajan gave him strict orders to clamp down on the places where rebellion commonly fomented.[18] At the time, any organization, even if it was just a volunteer fire department, was anathema to government authority, and was therefore banned. The local Christians had apparently chosen not to participate in the regular Roman civic festivities, meaning that local butchers and bakers were not selling as much meat and bread as before. Perhaps in a bid to get their businesses kick-started, they brought the Christians and their "secret meetings" to the attention of the authorities.

Pliny was perplexed. It is doubtful that he knew much about Christianity, but respectable citizens were bringing up their neighbors on charges of being part of a secret society that went by the name of "Christian." When Pliny asked the accused whether they were indeed Christians, they said yes. The accused thought they were simply acknowledging their faith, but according to Roman law, they were citing their allegiance to an illegal organization (again, because every non-Roman organization was illegal).[19] Roman justice was simple and swift.[20] If the arrested party was a Roman citizen, they were immediately bound and sent to Rome on the next boat; if not Roman, they were led out into the courtyard and executed.[21] But the people being brought in were not the criminal type. They were old

---

17. Plinius and Radice, *Letters of the Younger Pliny*, 17.
18. Pliny the Younger, *Letters*, 10.34.
19. Rives, "Persecution of Christians and Ideas of Community in the Roman Empire," 203.
20. W. H. C. Frend, *Martyrdom and Persecution in the Early Church*, 136.
21. Corke-Webster, "Trouble in Pontus," 382.

men, women, and even innocent girls. So Pliny wrote a letter to the emperor ostensibly asking for advice.

For many years this correspondence has been used by historians of all stripes to prove that Christianity was already illegal, and that Pliny was killing off Bithynian Christians wholesale. More modern scholarship, however, posits that Pliny had had enough of executing what few Christians he had been duped into killing already, and was looking for a way out. In his plea to Trajan, he suggests that Christians should no longer be sought after nor anonymously reported.[22] Trajan agreed.

No one knows how many Christians Pliny executed or dispatched to Rome for punishment, but no Christian source ever mentions the incident. And no other governor under Trajan ever reported mass Christian executions. Earlier scholars have assumed that what Trajan wrote to Pliny constituted Roman law from that time forth, and that if Christians, being members of a non-Roman organization, were reported in the right fashion, they could be executed. But even if Trajan's decree had been meant to be pervasive, it would not have been enduring, as edicts expired with the death of their issuer (unless explicitly renewed by the successor).[23]

Four or five other prominent Christians are purported to have been executed by the state under Trajan's reign, but most are of dubious attribution. The one we do have documentation for is Ignatius, bishop of Antioch. Eusebius does not report on the reason for his arrest, only that he was sent under "the strictest military surveillance" to Rome.[24] The actual surveillance must have been somewhat lax, for along the way Ignatius was apparently allowed to meet with, and write letters to, the bishops of various cities. His letters make it clear that Ignatius was a fire-eater, warning the church at Rome not to defend him, because he wanted to be "God's wheat, and by the teeth of wild beasts I am ground, that I may be found pure bread."[25] But, being a Roman citizen, he would not have been thrown to the lions, but beheaded. He would have known that, so his correspon-

22. Mary Beard, John North, and Simon Price, *Religions in Rome*, 237.
23. Corke-Webster, "Trouble in Pontus," 398.
24. Eusebius, *Church History*, 3.36.
25. Eusebius, *Church History*, 3.36.12.

dence about being eaten or burned is hyperbole. Whether he was actually executed is unknown. Irenaeus said he was, but he did not arrive in Rome until some fifty or sixty years later. The quote given to substantiate his martyrdom is simply another quote from one of Ignatius' letters—hardly an indicator of the actual method or reality of his death.[26] We can take Eusebius and Irenaeus at their word that Ignatius died at the hands of the imperial apparatus in Rome, but we cannot take for granted that Ignatius was executed simply for being a Christian. There is sufficient evidence to suppose him a voluntary martyr who did something against another Roman law that brought about his death. After all, none of his congregation, or any of those with whom he corresponded, was put to death.

### 4. Hadrian's Persecution (ca. 125 CE)

This persecution hardly bears mentioning, but since we have to enumerate the ten canonical persecutions, it must be cataloged. Five victims are identified by name, but except for Eustachius, an officer in the army, none can be verified. Foxe's *Book of Martyrs*, a highly questioned publication of Elizabethan England, tries to make the case that on two separate occasions a full 10,000 Christians were executed. But that wild claim has never been substantiated.

### 5. Marcus Aurelius' Persecution (circa 170 CE)

It was during the reign of this otherwise amenable emperor that the most tragic Christian deaths took place, accounting for at least fifty-five named victims including Bishop Polycarp, Justin Martyr, and eight victims of a hideous pogrom at Lugdunum (now Lyon, France) in 177 CE.

Polycarp has been mentioned several times in this book as being connected with John the apostle. His arrest, trial, and execution are documented by Eusebius in two separate accounts. That the man was taken and executed is clear. However, the story surrounding his demise is so embroidered with fanciful legends as to be of little value to the historian. We never get the Roman side of the story, only the breathless Christian account of his death. What is clear is

---

26. Eusebius, *Church History*, 3.36.12.

that, much like Jesus, his death can be attributed to a weak governor and an irate mob.[27]

One victim stands out as being a person we actually know *before* his death: an apologist whose works are cited in this book, Justin Martyr. Justin and a few Christian associates were tried and immediately beheaded in Rome for not complying with the decree to offer libations to Roman gods.[28] Historians have argued convincingly that the decree was not aimed at Christians, but at the Antonine Plague. It is thought that the plague came back with the legions from battles in Parthia that erupted when Marcus Aurelius took power and that it spread quickly among the legionnaires that had come down from as far away as Britannia.[29] Some historians think that the plague carried off "innumerable victims,"[30] up to 50 percent of the population, while others put the death toll at about 2 percent—perhaps as many as a million deaths.[31] The fear, paranoia, and social division that raged throughout Rome and its provinces, a society very much enamored with the supernatural, was only to be expected.[32] Therefore Marcus Aurelius issued an edict sometime between 161 and 167 CE directing all Roman citizens to sacrifice to the gods to help ameliorate the plague. Just as the victims of the fourteenth-century Great Mortality lashed out against Jews for poisoning wells, so did second-century Romans against those whom they saw as polluting the purity of their religious life and incurring the wrath of the gods. And, in this case, that included some Christians.

As brutal and merciless as were the fates of Justin, Polycarp, and their associates, the fate of the Gallic Martyrs is even more so. Eusebius includes in his history a letter from an anonymous person or persons who lived in Lugdunum in 177 CE recounting an awful pogrom that had just taken place. The victims include six men: Vetius, Sanctus, Biblias, Attalus, Pothnius, Ponticus; one woman: Blandina; and a youth: Alexander. The account details horrific and repeated tortures, under which none of the victims gave a hint of recanting

27. Thompson, "Martyrdom of Polycarp," 33.
28. Musurillo, *Acts of the Christian Martyrs*, 47.
29. Littman and Littman, "Galen and the Antonine Plague," 243.
30. Niebuhr, *Lectures on the History of Rome*, 733.
31. Gilliam, "Plague under Marcus Aurelius," 250.
32. Keresztes, "Marcus Aurelius a Prosecutor?," 332.

their faith. One man was even a Roman citizen, who should have been guaranteed a quick decapitation.[33]

But there are some problems with the account. For example, none of the Roman officials are named (something common in all other martyr stories),[34] the practices of both the Roman and Christian characters appear anachronistic,[35] and if one digs a little deeper, one can infer that both parties bore some of the blame. Also, the account details legal actions that are very suspect.[36] But the fact of the matter is that this was a lawless act perpetrated by a mob unconstrained by authorities. However, this was a singular case. No similar incident is reported until the Great Persecution more than 150 years later. So this cannot be held up as proof of systematic state-sponsored persecution of Christianity. It was an isolated event.

## 6. Severus' Persecution (ca. 200 CE)

Research reveals a list of thirty-three persons who are purported to have been Christian victims of Severus' Persecution. Historians agree that the trouble may be traced to an order that banned conversion to at least Judaism and perhaps Christianity.[37] Severus was apparently having a hard time staffing his army, partially because of Jewish draft dodgers.[38]

About ten of these victims died in Alexandria. However, the narrative of their martyrdom is supplied by partisan Christian scribes who write only of the piety and beauty of the victims, making no mention of their charges. This is strange because, except for the Gallic Martyrs, each person executed by the state would have had to have charges brought up by an accuser, be brought before the governor (no underlings), and be convicted. Stories that ignore those charges are suspect.

---

33. Eusebius, *Church History*, 5.1.1–63.

34. Anonymous, *Martyrdom of Polycarp*, 21; Anonymous, *Passion of the Scillitan Martyrs*.

35. Thompson, "Alleged Persecution of the Christians at Lyons in 177," 367, 373, 379.

36. Rives, "Persecution of Christians and Ideas of Community in the Roman Empire," 200.

37. Anonymous, *Historia Augusta: Septimius Severus*, 17.1.

38. Decret, *Early Christianity in North Africa*, 23.

Perhaps the most poignant and heart-rending martyr account is that of Perpetua, a young mother from Carthage (modern Tunis) imprisoned for weeks who then had her child ripped from her arms as she was led out naked to face the beasts and ultimately the sword. She was not alone; accounts name an additional eighteen persons who died around the same time in the same city. Many authors, modern and ancient, have held Perpetua up as a model of feminine piety and devotion, taking every word written in the anonymous account as pure gospel. [39] Others, however, have seen past the saccharine adulation to a deeply troubled woman. [40] Her judge gave her every opportunity to make amends and be released. Her father pleaded for her over and over again, even suffering a beating for her sake. She, however, clung to her fate.

It is true that thirty-three Christians felt it necessary to die for their faith during this time, but tens of thousands of their co-religionists did not. What was the difference? Whom should we hold up as exemplary? Whom shall we blame their deaths on?

### 7. Maximinius' Persecution (ca. 235 CE)

The number of victims attributed to Maximinus' time is nine, but, again, there is no mention of any particular decree or situation that would point to systemic persecution. Christian martyrologies are scarce on details and somewhat suspect. [41] In fact, of the seven ancient sources that catalog Christian persecutions, only one includes Maximinus. One suspects that he was added simply to round the number out to ten. But Maxinimius himself was an interesting guy.

Maximinus was a commoner who came from Thrace, and when you say "from Thrace" in Latin, it comes out "Thrax." Maximinus Thrax. I cannot help thinking of someone like a 260-pound linebacker for the Chicago Bears. And a linebacker he was. Long before his rise to power, he met the emperor Septimius Severus and begged to be admitted to the guard. To show his prowess, he wrestled sixteen of Severus' strongest guards, throwing them one by one. When the emperor rode away, Thrax trotted alongside the horse for miles,

---

39. Kitzler, "Passio Perpetuae and Acta Perpetuae," 17.
40. Hunink, "Did Perpetua Write Her Prison Account?," 148.
41. Clarke, "Some Victims of the Persecution of Maximinus Thrax," 446.

continuing his petition. When the emperor stopped, not even taking time to catch his breath, Thrax wrestled and beat seven more soldiers. The tales about the man go on, but most of them are probably as legendary as Paul Bunyan's.

### 8. Decius' Persecution (ca. 250 CE)

Throughout this recitation of canonical Christian persecutions, the named emperors did not have much to do with the said persecution—except for Nero. Decius is a different story. He actually issued an edict that had a direct and negative impact upon Christians throughout the empire.[42]

Decius came to power smack in the middle of the "Crisis of the Third Century," a time when the Roman Empire nearly suffered a total collapse.[43] Whereas the transfer of power from emperor to emperor was somewhat predictable for the empire's first two centuries, in the forty-six years previous to Decius' rise to power there had been at least twenty-six men who were proclaimed emperor, but whose actual reign was as short as twenty-one days. Enemy armies were attacking the empire from every direction, the currency was worthless, and food was scarce. Rome was retreating, and, for the first time since the ancient republic, it had to build walls to protect the city itself.[44]

Decius' predecessor to the throne was Philip, to whom Decius was a loyal public servant.[45] Philip sent him out with an army to quell one of the rebellions on the Danube River. After a swift victory, his adoring soldiers hoisted Decius on a shield and proclaimed him *imperator,* probably in a calculated effort to get cash bonuses and cushy assignments back in Rome.[46] Decius went along with the charade, marched back to Rome, killed Philip, and took the throne. Since he had no tenable claim to the throne, his immediate job was to consolidate power so that he could establish a dynasty. But he was killed less

---

42. Robinson, *Criminal Law of Ancient Rome,* 556.

43. Alföldy, "Crisis of the Third Century as Seen by Contemporaries," 90.

44. Dey, *Aurelian Wall and the Refashioning of Imperial Rome,* 111; Southern, *Roman Empire from Severus to Constantine,* 120.

45. Potter, *Prophecy and History in the Crisis of the Roman Empire,* 40.

46. Potter, *Prophecy,* 41.

than two years later in a battle along the Danube River in modern Bulgaria, becoming the first Roman emperor to die in battle.[47]

Before he headed off to battle, however, he issued an edict requiring that every Roman citizen offer a sacrifice to the gods and pledge allegiance to the new emperor. At least we think this is what they had to do since no copy of the edict is extant.[48] To give his decree some teeth, he apparently specified that one had to be able to show a certificate of compliance, or a *libelli*. It is from these *libelli* that we have deduced the edict's existence.

Christian authors have long held that the edict was addressed to Christians, and that they were being forced to sacrifice to Roman gods.[49] Decius, however, did not specify which gods should receive the sacrifices. Local gods were as acceptable as the Roman pantheon. No pagan worship was being demanded, just participation in the civic sacrificial tradition.[50] That the edict was issued specifically to Christians has been repudiated by the *libelli*. When one analyzes the names from the *libelli*, only a few of them are obviously Christian names: Theodore, Dioscorus, and Thecla. The remainder of the names are non-Christian, for example Aurelia Ammonous, who was an Egyptian priestess.[51]

The number of Christians who perished because of Decius' edict is unknown, though Foxe's gory and undocumented account puts the death toll at about forty from all over the empire.[52] But forty hardly comprises a significant fraction of Christians living in the empire at the time, which may have numbered from 500,000 to 1 million.[53] Obviously there were many, many more Christians who, finding a way to justify the sacrifice as more of a pledge of allegiance than

---

47. Potter, *Roman Empire at Bay*, 245.

48. Rives, "Decree of Decius and the Religion of Empire," 136.

49. Rives, "Decree," 151.

50. Beard, North, and Price, *Religions of Rome*, 239

51. Knipfing, "Libelli of the Decian Persecution," 359–361.

52. John Foxe, chap. 2 in *Acts and Monuments*.

53. Stark, *Cities of God*, 67. Stark starts with a population of 1,000 Christians in 50 CE and applies a conversion/birth annual growth rate of 3.4 percent, arriving at 1.12 million Christians by 250 CE. Stark notes that a 3.4 percent rate has been consistently documented by the Jehovah's Witnesses and the LDS Church in modern times. He does not take into account the plagues that affected the empire during the intervening years, which may have halved that amount.

outright apostasy, found a way to live in harmony with the emperor's decree in an effort to return Rome to its former security and glory.

## 9. Valerian's Persecution (255 CE)

Valerian came to power a scant two years after Decius died in battle, but during that time there had been three other emperors. Wars had not abated, and what's more, a virulent plague was ravaging the populace and devastating the economy.[54] But amid all this, there are reports that Valerian was a pretty good friend of the Christians.[55] But one of his staff, Macrianus, was not. As a result of Macrianus' influence, Valerian in 257 CE sent an order to the senate in Rome and perhaps directly to provincial governors. No direct artifact of the *rescript* is extant, but descriptions by both Dionysius and Cyprian say that it asked Christian leaders to "acknowledge the Roman rites."[56] The penalties for disobedience included being sent to work in the mines or being exiled to a city outside one's bishopric.[57] This mild mandate was, however, quickly followed up by another one stating that church officials (not regular church members) who would not sacrifice would be executed.[58] Why would a friend of the church turn against them? It may well be that Macrianus, who clearly had influence over Valerian, wanted to fill the war chest.

Note the use of a word in the previous paragraph that had not yet been used in this chapter: church. By the middle of the third century CE, the community of Christians had grown into a property-holding corporation that built churches and cemeteries, perhaps not on par with Roman temples yet, but at least stand-alone structures with a little sign out front that said, "Visitors Welcome." In other words, the church had money. And Macrianus needed money to fund the wars in Persia.

Macrianus' edicts were not so much a persecution of the saints as a money grab. This was not an uncommon practice in Roman politics.

---

54. Pontius the Deacon, *Life and Passion of St. Cyprian*; Harper, "People, Plagues, and Prices in the Roman World," 806.

55. Eusebius, *Church History*, 7.10.3.

56. Musurillo, *Acts of the Christian Martyrs*, 169.

57. Keresztes, "Two Edicts of the Emperor Valerian," 84; Millar, *Emperor in the Roman World*, 569.

58. Keresztes, "Two Edicts," 90, 94.

In both 82 BCE, under Sulla, and 43 BCE, under Augustus, similar things happened. Under the guise of getting rid of enemies of the state, both leaders had posted some names for quick apprehension and execution. Whoever ratted on the person was given a portion of the proscripted man's wealth, but the bulk of his estate went to refilling the state's coffers that had been depleted by civil wars.[59]

The documented death toll in this case comes to thirty-three men, all of them church leaders, including Sixtus II, the bishop of Rome, and several of his assistants. Also executed was the notable Cyprian, bishop of Carthage, who wrote much and played a pivotal role in North African church history. The undocumented list of those sent to mines is perhaps much longer.

Valerian, however, became a much more notable casualty. Whereas Decius had been killed in battle, Valerian was taken captive in a loss to the Persians. Later Christian authors, wanting to denigrate such a vile persecutor of the church, wrote that the emperor was kept in a cage and forced to become a human footstool any time the Persian Shah wanted to mount his horse. When he died, his corpse was stuffed and displayed in the Shah's hall.[60] Valerian's son succeeded to the throne peacefully and almost immediately issued an official relief for the Christians, restoring their property.[61]

## 10. Diocletian's Persecution (ca. 305 CE)

During the fifty years that transpired between Valerian's death and Diocletian's ascent to the throne in 284 CE, things were going swimmingly for the Christians. Church members had risen to prominence in the government and military. The church had become so rich that it had built a chapel right across the street from one of the emperors' palaces—and it was every bit as tall. But around 302 CE, Christians within the government were accused of making Christian gestures at Roman religious ceremonies. This made Diocletian upset. In February the next year, it had gotten so bad that the big church near the palace was looted and demolished. The next day Diocletian and Galerius issued a joint edict that made practicing Christianity illegal,

---

59. Keaveney, *Sulla Dictator*, 126; Syme, *Roman Revolution*, 192.
60. Potter, *Roman Empire*, 256.
61. Eusebius, *Church History*, 7.13.

mandating the destruction of churches and scriptures, and the imprisonment of church leaders who did not comply. Over the course of the next couple of years, three more orders were issued, each more stringent that the last, ultimately calling for the execution of certain Christians. These years are traditionally called the Great Persecution.

Eusebius, who wrote *Church History*, also wrote another work called *The Martyrs of Palestine*. During the time of the Great Persecution, he was a high official of the church in Caesarea Maritima, the capital of the Province of Palaestina, located on the Israeli coast halfway between Tel Aviv and Haifa. Since this was where the governor lived, and a governor was the only one who could pass a death sentence, Eusebius was on hand to detail the deaths of forty-eight individuals, doing his best to recount the reason for their arrest and the manner of their demise (all gruesome). Only three men and one woman remain nameless. He also enumerates a hundred Egyptians who were killed all at once, and forty nameless men who were killed in a copper mine, although these two incidents have less documentation.

And this was just in Palestine. There were roughly 120 provinces in the Roman Empire at the time. Scholars have debated how many people died during this time. One came up with a number, not of victims, but of persecutions—about 93.[62] However, another historian criticizes his use of martyrologies and dismisses the large number.[63] Interestingly, all the persecutions occurred in the eastern half of the Roman Empire. In the north, it seems that the emperor in Italy did not want to have anything to do with them. Perhaps it had something to do with his having a Christian wife. His reluctance may have contributed to the path of his son Constantine the Great, who would roll back Diocletian's persecution as soon as he came to power in 313 CE. Taking all this into account, how many victims were there of the persecutions? We will never know on this side of the veil, but my estimate comes to around 5,000.

But when we look at Eusebius' Palestinian account, we see that an overwhelming number of these were what he labeled "voluntary martyrs." For example, Procopius, who was required to make an offering to the gods when entering the city, refused and was immediately

---

62. Davies, "Origin and Purpose of the Persecution of AD 303," 68–69.
63. Corcoran, "Before Constantine," 36.

beheaded. Zacchaeus was in prison on anti-Christian charges, but when he was let out, he refused to relent, for which recalcitrance he was tortured and killed. Alphaeus saw some condemned Christians being led to their death and jumped in with them. Romanus did the same, and although the magistrate cut out his tongue instead of killing him, he continued his civil disobedience until he was finally dispatched. The list goes on.[64] We are tempted to congratulate these martyrs on their dedication to their Christian faith, but Christians had been admonished by the Lord to "render unto Caesar the things that are Caesar's" and by Paul to get along with their overlords, just as Latter-day Saints have been admonished to uphold the law of the land. As Paul wrote:

> Let every person be subject to the governing authorities. For there is no authority except by God's appointment, and the authorities that exist have been instituted by God. So the person who resists such authority resists the ordinance of God, and those who resist will incur judgment (for rulers cause no fear for good conduct but for bad). Do you desire not to fear authority? Do good and you will receive its commendation because it is God's servant for your well-being. But be afraid if you do wrong because government does not bear the sword for nothing. It is God's servant to administer punishment on the person who does wrong. Therefore it is necessary to be in subjection, not only because of the wrath of the authorities but also because of your conscience. For this reason you also pay taxes, for the authorities are God's servants devoted to governing. Pay everyone what is owed: taxes to whom taxes are due, revenue to whom revenue is due, respect to whom respect is due, honor to whom honor is due. (Rom. 13:1–7, NET.)

Hundreds of thousands of Christians during this time found a way to co-exist with their Roman neighbors by participating in their civil ceremonies, which were probably as religious as a 4th of July parade and barbeque. Those who did die seemed to be actively pursuing martyrdom—maybe not be the kind of people we should revere and emulate. In the LDS Church, there are no prohibitions on attending the services of other denominations, faiths, or religions. We may participate in them every bit as much as we allow others to participate in our own. Just as we do not expect our visitors to

---

64. Eusebius, *Martyrs*, 1.

partake of the bread and water in our sacrament, neither would we partake of the bread and wine at their service, not because it is unholy, but because we are not members of their covenant.

Whatever notion you had about Christian martyrs before you read this chapter, I hope now that you will recognize that their number is probably much smaller that you initially imagined, that martyrdom was not the only course their lives could have taken, and that we can learn from them not to be so steeped in a narrow interpretation of our own doctrine that we cannot reach out and experience the worship of others.

# THE WORLD WAS PLUNGED INTO THE DARK AGES

It has long been the practice of historians to divide world history into discrete boxes with easily identifiable names. This gives the impression that human development has proceeded in an orderly advance. For example, we start with the Stone Age (up to about 3000 BCE), followed by the Bronze Age (3000–1200 BCE), and then on to the Iron Age (1200 BCE–300 BCE). Things get a little messier after that with different eras cropping in different locations with overlapping times. Up until the last generation, most historians used familiar labels to describe Europe after the "Fall of Rome." No doubt, you have heard them before: Renaissance, Reformation, and Enlightenment. Each of these terms describes an era of growth and rediscovery after what had been a supposedly stifling and uninteresting thousand-year period called the "Dark Ages."

It turns out that the term Dark Ages was invented by one of the leading lights of the Renaissance, Francesco Petrarca (or Petrarch, 1304–74 CE). He looked around at the ruins in Italy and figured that the thousand years between the Fall of Rome and himself had been nothing but darkness and barbarism.[1] Do not get me wrong. I idolize Petrarch and all his Renaissance siblings. The last time I visited his stomping grounds in Florence, Italy, I geeked out on every other street corner with this piece of art, that person's home, or another famous church. But even if, to Petrarch, dark meant "unknown" rather than "worthless," he was straight-up wrong.

That the Dark Ages were not so dark does not detract from

---

1. Petrarch, *On His Own Ignorance and That of Many Others*, 45; Theodor Mommsen, "Petrarch's Conception of the 'Dark Ages,'" 227.

the amazing advances in art, architecture, language, and learning wrought by the many geniuses who called fifteenth-century Tuscany home. We can still gawk at Michelangelo's *David* and *Pietà*; Leonardo's art and inventions can still amaze us; and we can climb Brunelleschi's Dome to heart-stopping exhaustion and views, but we need to recognize the achievements of their forebears in what is better called the medieval period.

Latter-day Saints are unfortunately even guiltier than Petrarch in discounting this period. Although it has begun to change in the several decades since general authorities such as Elders Monson, Packer, and Hinckley have made mention of people like Wyclif and Tyndale in conference addresses, the average elder, sister, or otherwise knows little of, and gives less credit to, anything between Peter's demise and Brother Joseph's miraculous manifestations.[2]

A quick Google search for "were the dark ages really dark?" brings up pages from Quora and the History Channel (among others) that will tell you that historians no longer think that calling it the "Dark Ages" is proper. They prefer "medieval." However, that term has been co-opted to mean brutally barbaric, hardly helpful. However, these pages will point out several advancements you might not be aware of that happened during the "Dark Ages."

Note, for example, the agricultural developments of the heavy plow and the horse collar, although credit must go to the Han Chinese for the plow. The horse collar allowed a horse to pull a heavier load than even an ox could handle. The heavy plow could actually turn a furrow in the ground instead of just scratching up the surface. In tandem, these two inventions led to thriving agriculture where only small gardens and grazing had taken place before.[3] Combine this with an unusually good climate between 950 and 1250 CE, and we get many healthy, vigorous, and even *tall* people. It might not seem much to modern farmers who can watch Netflix in air-conditioned comfort while plowing a field the size of Denmark, but since

---

2. Thomas S. Monson, "The Way Home," *Ensign*, May 1975; Monson, "They Showed the Way," *Ensign*, May 1997; Gordon B. Hinckley, "At the Summit of the Ages," *Ensign*, Nov. 1999; D. Todd Christofferson, "The Blessing of the Scriptures," *Ensign*, May 2010; Boyd K. Packer, "Under the Direction of the Holy Spirit," *Ensign*, May 2011.

3. Thomas et al., *"Technology, Ritual and Anglo-Saxon Agriculture,"* 742–58.

Adam and Eve taught Abel to grow radishes, no one had ever gotten beyond an ox-drawn scratch plow.

Meanwhile, those who were not brawny enough to drive horses back and forth across the fields all day got their parent's permission to go live in a monastery for the rest of their lives. They became monks and nuns, but their lives were not any easier. When they were not growing their own radishes, they were keeping literacy alive across Europe. They read the few great books the monastery owned and copied out new versions of them, sometimes adding a flourish or opinion here or there. They also taught rich people's children. Being literate, these children became the secretaries of state, prosecuting attorneys, and financial exchequers of the illiterate kings and princes. Over time, in places like Paris, Bologna, and Oxford, these monasteries developed into the first universities. The very idea of what a scholastic curriculum should consist of originated with Boethius, a Roman nobleman of the sixth century CE (after the "Fall of Rome"), and consisted of what we still call the seven liberal arts. Where education in Roman times consisted of memorizing prose and poetry, and learning arithmetic, Boethius and Gerbert (later Pope Sylvester II) expanded it to include astronomy, mathematics, geometry, and music (the *quadrivium*) and joined them with the artistic disciplines of rhetoric, grammar, and logic (the *trivium*). This was part of the movement that has culminated in modern education.[4]

Another note in your Google search would be that science, math, and medicine got a huge boost during this time. And it would properly give credit to the Arabs for having done so. Were it not for the brilliant minds of Ibn Sina (Avicenna), Ibn Rushd (Averroës), and Ibn al–Nadīm, not to mention several of their Jewish counterparts such as Maimonides and Moses ben Nahman, we might still be corralling horses to plow our fields.[5]

I cannot leave the discussion of the "Dark Ages" without devoting a few more words on the above-named Boethius. Some four centuries after the apostles had left their ministries, this man still had access to enough truth to write a brilliant and moving book called *The Consolation of Philosophy*, a book that C. S. Lewis (the darling of

4. Herman, *Cave and the Light*, 210.
5. Herman, *Cave*, 244.

many LDS intelligentsia, not to mention general authorities) called one of the ten most influential books he had ever read.[6] Boethius, who had reached the pinnacle of success in family and community, was falsely denounced by his former friend and colleagues, sent to prison, and eventually strangled. While awaiting the garrote, he penned the alternating poetry and prose of this delightful, moving, and heart-rending dialogue between himself and an allegorical embodiment of knowledge, a Greek goddess type character named *Sophia*.[7] Its basic gist is that nothing is of any real value except the truth. My copy is an audio book narrated by the silken-voiced David Rintoul. I was in the midst of listening to this masterpiece when I suddenly and unexpectedly lost my work-at-home software development job during the onset of the COVID-19 pandemic. I can testify that it was the ideas communicated by Boethius a millennium and half ago that prepared me to meet that devastating news with a constructive attitude.

Perhaps the culmination of the advances of the "Dark Ages" is encapsulated in the great twelfth and thirteenth-century cathedrals of France and Germany. Take, for example Cathédrale Notre-Dame de Chartres, the Kölner Dom, the York Minster, and of course Cathédrale Notre Dame de Paris. These soaring filigrees of stone, glass, and air are marvels of construction whose architectural methods and concepts, though well understood, are still somewhat of a mystery. Even with modern construction tools and materials, the Washington DC National Cathedral (classified as neo–Gothic, complete with flying buttresses and gargoyles) took 83 years to complete. Indeed, the methods used to create the original stained glass of Chartres are unknown today.

Perhaps my personal experience with the Kölner Dom can be the final illustration of this chapter's point. As a young boy, my father was stationed in Germany as part of the US Army Europe. During those four years my parents dragged us kids away from our friends

---

6. John G. West, "Top Ten Books That Influenced C.S. Lewis," *C.S. Lewis Web*, Aug. 2, 2012.

7. Philosophy in Boethius's day meant all knowledge, not just metaphysics or epistemology.

on long weekends and forced us to traipse through a seemingly endless procession of castles, churches, and ruins.

I specifically remember visiting the Cathedral in Cologne (or Köln), looking at the gold-covered, overly ornate altars and endless smoke-stained pillars and saying to myself, "What a waste! All of this wealth could have been given to the poor!" I felt that these cathedrals were monstrosities, indeed, that they were houses of the devil. It certainly was not an original thought; I think it was, in fact, the prevailing Mormon mindset at the time.

Luckily, I had the opportunity to revisit that same cathedral as a newly minted adult while on tour with my college choir. With fresh eyes, I entered the Kölner Dom. Much of the blackness, which I had assumed was the natural color of the stone, but which was due to air pollution over the 800 years of the building's life, had been cleaned away. Music came from a recording of a boys' choir. Crepuscular rays of sunlight filtered in from windows some fifty yards overhead, giving the effect of heavenly visions upon the congregants below.

New visions began to appear through the newly opened windows of my own mind. Yes, the altar was still ornate and covered with gold, but the funds to pay for the art had not been extorted from the populace; it was a treasure they had freely given. The smoke on the interior columns was not so much from coal dust as candle wax, representing the millions of prayers that had been offered up by my fellow humans over centuries to the same God I called upon. Although I have heard some Latter-day Saints opine that a prayer offered by a Catholic to a saint is as effective as praying to a garbage can, I now knew otherwise. The prayers of the gnarled old women who gathered here daily, who had lost their sons and husbands in WWII and now lived lives of crushing loneliness, were precious in the sight of their Lord in whose name they incessantly crossed themselves. I can honestly say that on that May afternoon of 1987 my understanding of the Lord's plan of salvation, which I had taught expertly on my LDS mission, was opened up and illuminated as had been promised me in my patriarchal blessing years before.

The Lord's work did not suddenly cease in 95 CE. God was not silent for 1,725 years. God's intelligence was pouring down endlessly in many, many places.

# THE GREAT AND ABOMINABLE
# CHURCH IS A CHURCH

In 1958 Bruce R. McConkie, then a member of the First Quorum of the Seventy of the LDS Church, wrote in his first edition of *Mormon Doctrine*:

> *Church of the Devil.* There are two scriptural senses in which the titles *church of the devil* and *great and abominable church* are used: 1. All churches or organizations of whatever name or nature—whether political, philosophical, educational, economic, social, fraternal, civic, or religious— which are designed to take men on a course that leads away from God and his laws and thus from salvation in the kingdom of God; and 2. The *Roman Catholic Church* specifically—singled out, set apart, described, and designated as being "most abominable above all other churches."[1]

I am not a historian of Mormonism, so I do not know the whole story behind the first edition of *Mormon Doctrine*, but I do know that it was almost immediately censured. The second edition arrived after eight years of revisions, and it had a much less dogmatic foreword that included the slightly chastened phrase "experience has shown the wisdom of making some changes, clarifications, and additions." The damage was done, however. A generation of Latter-day Saints now read Nephi's description of "gold, and silver, and silks, and scarlets, and fine-twined linen, and ... many harlots" (1 Ne. 13:7) as the pomp and circumstance of the Roman Catholic Church. And Elder McConkie did not back down in the second edition from his intolerant stance against any religion other than the LDS Church. "There is no salvation outside this one true church, the Church of Jesus Christ," he intoned. "Any church or organization which satisfied the

---

1. McConkie, *Mormon Doctrine*, 129.

innate religious longings of a man and keeps him from coming to the saving truths of Christ and his gospel is therefore not of God."[2] For him, the church of Christ is comprised *only* of the Church of Jesus Christ of Latter-day Saints.

Elder McConkie's influence on LDS thought exposes a hole in our understanding of the apostasy. The devil's church is not one church; it is not limited to churches; and it is not limited to Europe. Kent Jackson affirms that if Latter-day Saints imagine medieval monks tampering with the scriptures or the Catholic Church's pomp and circumstance to be the antecedent of Nephi's description, they are wrong. In particular defense of the scribes and monks, he points out that Nephi says that the plain and precious things would be taken out of the gospel *before* it went to the world.[3]

There certainly have been corrupt popes among the more than 250 men who have carried that title.[4] For example, when Giovanni di Lorenzo de' Medici was elected Pope Leo X in 1513 CE, he is reputed to have said, "God has given us the papacy, now let us enjoy it," although this quote's authenticity has been disputed. Nonetheless, although several of his direct predecessors (such as della Rovera and de Borja) were worldly and suspect, it was de' Medici's actions that finally pushed Martin Luther over the edge. Many popes, however, were honestly and sincerely in it solely for the welfare of the church and the glory of God. Two such men were Gregorius Anicius (590–604 CE) and Angelo Giuseppe Roncalli (1958–63 CE), respectively Gregory I "the Great" and John XXIII "the Blessed." Not only were they humble and devoted men, but they were supremely effective in leading the church both spiritually and temporally. Gregory, who was the first monk ever to be made pope, saved his people from marauding bandits and sold papal property to help feed the people, while also founding missions in as yet non-Christian northern Europe (such as Canterbury, the seat of the English church today).[5] John is held as the most beloved, ecumenical, and open-hearted pope in history, who deftly brought about the Second Vatican Council that began

---

2. McConkie, *Mormon Doctrine*, 138.
3. Jackson, *From Apostasy to Restoration*, 20–21.
4. As of this writing, Pope Francis is serving as the 266th named pope.
5. McBrien, *Lives of the Popes*, 17.

the process of bringing the church, occasionally kicking and scream-
ing, into the modern world. His encyclical *Pacem in terris*, addressed
not only to Catholic bishops and their parishioners, but to the entire world, was called "the voice and conscience of the world" by the
*Washington Post*.[6] And let us not forget that LDS Apostle L. Tom
Perry actually quoted Pope Francis in a general conference address.[7]

In other words, while some who sat upon the Bishop of Rome's
seat may have been unworthy, others who sat there might be found
today standing next to Brother Joseph's older brother, Alvin, in
heaven (D&C 137:5–7). It is people, not institutions, who comprise
the devil's church. Understanding this, it is unproductive to try to
identify the church of the devil. Why search for darkness when so
much light surrounds us? We should look for members of the church
of Christ, not acolytes of Satan. Especially when we finally break out
of our Eurocentric tendencies and discover the extraordinary band-
width the Light of Christ manifests all over the world.

When we focus only on European aspects of Christianity, we miss
denominations in places like Armenia, Egypt, India, and China. And
then limiting the discussion to Christianity robs us of the offerings
of faiths like Judaism, Islam, Hinduism, Buddhism, and Sikhism.
When we leave our white, Eurocentric focus and consider God's
workings among peoples elsewhere in the world, we discover how
wide the membership of the church of Christ really is. While Elder
McConkie might believe that Hindus do not possess even an iota
of truth, for example, is it not possible that when the resurrected
Jesus told the Nephites he had to go visit other sheep, that people
on the Indian subcontinent were among them, and that the Indian
religions were informed by that visit? Perhaps we Latter-day Saints
could spend some time learning the truths passed down through
Hinduism so that we would be able to better converse with the Indians who cross our path in the growing global economy. Perhaps
Muhammad was indeed visited by Gabriel and given a message that
benefited the people of his place and time.[8]

---

6. J. J. Ziegler, "Pacem in Terris at 50," *The Catholic World Report*, June 14, 2013.

7. L. Tom Perry, "Why Marriage and Family Matter—Everywhere in the World,"
*Ensign*, May 2015.

8. James E. Faust, "Communion with the Holy Spirit," *Ensign*, May 1980.

We may be as misguided as the young John, who, when he encountered a miracle worker not associated with Jesus, said, "Teacher,
we saw someone driving out demons in your name and we told him
to stop, because he was not one of us." To which Jesus replied, "Do
not stop him, for no one who does a miracle in my name can in the
next moment say anything bad about me, *for whoever is not against us
is for us.* Truly I tell you, anyone who gives you a cup of water in my
name because you belong to the Messiah will certainly not lose their
reward." (Mark 9:38–41; emphasis mine). The membership of church
of Christ is bigger, wider, longer, and deeper that we can imagine.

We have seen in the pages of this book that many of the ideas we
have acquired about the great apostasy are incorrect traditions that
have come to us through our forebears (Alma 3:8, 11). In the past we
have used these traditions to build up a barrier between us and the
world. We sought to become a peculiar people. At the time, perhaps
these traditions were tares allowed to spring up within the field of
wheat because the wheat was yet too tender (D&C 86:6). The efforts of LDS Church presidents like Gordon B. Hinckley, Thomas
S. Monson, and Russell M. Nelson have shown us that such a time
is past. It is time for the Latter-day Saints to take their place *among*
the world—not apart from it; and certainly not above it.

As the Doctrine and Covenants reminds us:

> Therefore, I will unfold unto [those who don't yet understand the scrip-
> tures] this great mystery; for behold, I will gather them as a hen gathers
> her chickens under her wings, if they will not harden their hearts; yea,
> if they will come, they may partake of the waters of life freely. Behold,
> this is my doctrine—whosoever repents and comes unto me, the same
> is *in my church.* Whoever declares more or less than this, the same is not
> of me, but is against me; therefore, he is not in my church. And now,
> behold, whoever is of my church, and endures of my church to the end,
> they will I establish upon my rock, and the gates of hell shall not prevail
> against them. (D&C 10:64–69; English modernization added.)

The requirements for becoming part of the Lord's church are to re-
pent and come unto him. Are the waters of life necessarily baptism
by the authority of the Aaronic Priesthood into the Church of Jesus
Christ of Latter-day Saints? No, that is the requirement we Saints
believe opens the door to the celestial kingdom, not to become part

of the Lord's church. Anyone who is of the church and remains in the church is established upon the rock.

Let us leave behind the false traditions of our fathers and mothers that deny the goodness and grace of God that has guided and still guides the faith of many of our friends and neighbors. In the conclusion to this book, I suggest an alternate script for explaining the great apostasy. Let us leave behind the declarations that jump from Jesus to Joseph, that denigrate and dismiss the work of the Lord in bringing about the many different paths that lead to him, and from him to the Father. Let us acknowledge that the Lord's prophesy to Peter that his rock, his church, would never vanish from the earth was, indeed, true. It is bigger and wider and deeper than the Latter-day Saints, and we would do well to know of the goodness of Jesus to all his siblings (Morm. 1:15).

CONCLUSION

# THE GREAT APOSTASY
# FOR LATTER-DAY SAINTS

For thousands of years God has sent his children to live here on Earth to learn to love and follow him. In humanity's earliest days, God had but one name and message, which was proclaimed by special people, or prophets. Like all people in every dispensation, the knowledge of God faded behind the everyday struggle to survive. God never stops loving his children, and he never stops calling to them through prophets. Every land has had them—people who try to reveal the right way to live. Although they have called God by different names and explained the purpose of life somewhat differently, every true prophet teaches a message that leads people to live a more just and equitable life.

Latter-day Saints believe that about 2,000 years ago a unique prophet was sent from God with a message that restored the true knowledge of God. We believe he was not only a prophet, but had a special aspect of divinity that gave him more power and authority than any prophet before or after him. Indeed we believe he was so special that God chose him to do a work for all of humanity that we could not do for ourselves: to give us the means to overcome all our problems in this life and eventually become perfected. During his life, he was known as Yeshua bar Yusef, but because he fulfilled many ancient prophecies, he was called the *Anointed One*, which word in the most widely spoken language in his area (Greek) was *Kristos*. His name is now spoken differently in many tongues. Christians call him Jesus Christ.

Jesus lived an exemplary life, taught a glorious gospel, and gathered such a following that his local political leaders began to fear him. He was arrested, tried, and executed by crucifixion. We believe that this was part of God's plan—that Jesus died to be an atoning sacrifice for our transgressions. A few days after his death, he was seen alive again. During the next forty days, he met with his most devoted followers, his apostles. He explained things they had not understood before. These special teachings were not written in the Gospels, but remained personal and sacred to the apostles. The teachings endowed them with knowledge and power to work miracles and to stand as witnesses before mobs and rulers. The apostles dispersed throughout the known world preaching Jesus' gospel from Europe to India. They conveyed this gospel with power and authority. They passed not only their truth, but their power and authority to new converts. Some apostles were killed for preaching the gospel, but, as Jesus promised his chief apostle, the church founded by the apostles has endured for two millennia. The gates of hell have menaced against it, and at times the church has been almost overpowered, but Christianity remains today as one of the world's greatest religions.

However, beginning just a few generations after the apostles and their successors had died, people started to mix their own ideas with gospel truths. People who converted to Christianity brought their own traditions with them, sometimes causing cultural disunity within the church. Some men sought to gain their own power and authority, instead of seeking to serve humbly with God's power and authority. Some wanted money and prestige; others wanted to attract followers. Jesus had warned about such people. He called them sheep in wolves' clothing. Despite the warnings, people were persuaded to follow their teachings. Eventually some of what Jesus had taught was either lost or changed. The community that Jesus had established was not dead, but people became estranged into groups that followed different teachings. Each group had mostly the same scriptures and taught the same basic gospel, but they let their human-made differences divide them.

Although the truth of God's word was found in their scriptures, God raised up prophets again and again to remind people of what was truly good and what was human-made. Some of them revealed new scriptures. Others brought the scriptures they already had back into clear focus. We do not know all their names, nor is it clear to what extent God revealed his message to them. But through various ways and means, God kept trying to lead his children to live just and equitable lives.

Some two centuries ago, God brought another prophet with power and authority to restore Jesus' message and community. That prophet's calling came as he read God's word in his home and prayed to God in a forest.

This latter-day prophet looked around him and saw truth and goodness in many different denominations because prophets before him had labored to preserve and renew fading or lost truths. But this new prophet knew there had to be a single truth that united them all. And because of yet another prophet who taught that God could be found not just in church, but also in nature, the new prophet did not try to resolve his question in a church building; he found his way into the solitude of a forest where he prayed from his heart.

A miracle happened in that forest that day. God manifested himself to that prophet. Soon, the prophet established a community of followers to whom God revealed long-lost truths and gave power and authority to share these truths with the world. That community is today called the Church of Jesus Christ of Latter-day Saints. We believe we latter-day saints are inheritors of the gospel preached by Jesus and his apostles—not only that which has been published in his Gospels, but that which he taught to his apostles after he was raised from the dead. It is a gospel full of plain and precious truths, some of which were lost but now restored. We believe that living this gospel can help God's children live a more just and equitable life, eventually perfecting us so that we may return to God some day. We do not question or doubt the truths and goodness found in the world's other religions. We simply offer our testimony as a part of God's love for and continuing revelation to his children.

# Bibliography

## Primary Sources

Anonymous. *Didache*. Translated by M. B. Riddle. In *Ante-Nicene Fathers*, edited by Alexander Roberts, James Donaldson, and A. Cleveland Coxe, vol. 7. Buffalo, NY: Christian Literature Publishing Co., 1886. See *New Advent*, accessed Sep. 6, 2021, www.newadvent.org/fathers/0714.htm.

Anoymous. *Epistle of Clement to James*. Translated by James Donaldson. In *Ante-Nicene Christian Library: Translations of the Writings of the Fathers Down to A.D. 325*, edited by Alexander Roberts and James Donaldson, vol. 17. Edinburgh: T. & T. Clark, 1870. See *Bible Study Tools*, accessed Aug. 20, 2021, www.biblestudytools.com.

Anonymous. *Epistle of Peter to James*. Translated by James Donaldson. In *Ante-Nicene Christian Library: Translations of the Writings of the Fathers Down to A.D. 325*, edited by Alexander Roberts and James Donaldson, vol. 17. Edinburgh: T. & T. Clark, 1870. See *The Tertullian Project*, accessed Aug. 20, 2021, www.tertullian.org/fathers2/ANF-08/anf08-42.htm.

Anonymous. *Historia Augusta*. Translated by David Magie. Cambridge, MA: Harvard University Press, 1921. See *LacusCurtius*, accessed Sep. 6, 2021, www.penelope.uchicago.edu/Thayer/E/Roman/Texts/Historia_Augusta.

Anonymous. *Liber Pontificalis*. Translated by Louise Ropes Loomis. New York: Columbia University Press, 1916.

Anonymous. *Teaching of Addaeus the Apostle*. Translated by B.P. Pratten. In *Ante-Nicene Fathers*, edited by Alexander Roberts, James Donaldson, and A. Cleveland Coxe, vol. 8. Buffalo, NY: Christian Literature Publishing Co., 1886. See *New Advent*, accessed Sep. 6, 2021, www.newadvent.org/fathers/0853.htm.

Anonymous. *The Teaching of the Apostles*. Translated by B. P. Pratten. In *Ante-Nicene Fathers*, edited by Alexander Roberts, James Donaldson, and A. Cleveland Coxe, vol. 8. Buffalo, NY: Christian Literature Publishing Co., 1886. See *New Advent*, accessed Aug. 9, 2021, www.newadvent.org/fathers/0854.htm.

Anonymous. *The Martyrdom of Polycarp*. Translated by Alexander Roberts and James Donaldson. In *Ante-Nicene Fathers*, edited by Alexander Roberts, James Donaldson, and A. Cleveland Coxe, vol. 1. Buffalo, NY: Christian Literature Publishing Co., 1885. See *New Advent*, accessed Aug. 9, 2021, www.newadvent.org/fathers/0102.htm.

Anonymous. *The Passion of the Scillitan Martyrs.* Translated by J. Armitage Robinson. In *Ante-Nicene Fathers*, edited by Allan Menzies, vol. 9. Buffalo, NY: Christian Literature Publishing Co., 1896. See *New Advent*, accessed Aug. 9, 2021, www.newadvent.org/fathers/1013.htm.

Clement of Alexandria. *Stromata.* Translated by William Wilson. In *Ante-Nicene Fathers,* edited by Alexander Roberts, James Donaldson, and A. Cleveland Coxe, vol. 2. Buffalo, NY: Christian Literature Publishing Co., 1885. See *New Advent*, accessed Aug. 10, 2021, www.newadvent.org/fathers/0210.htm.

Clement of Rome. *Epistle to the Corinthians.* Translated by John Keith. In *Ante-Nicene Fathers*, edited by Allan Menzies, vol. 9. Buffalo, NY: Christian Literature Publishing Co., 1886. See *New Advent,* accessed Aug. 10, 2021, www.newadvent.org/fathers/1010.htm.

Cyprian. *On Baptism, Against the Donatists.* Translated by J. R. King. In *Nicene and Post-Nicene Fathers*, First Series, edited by Philip Schaff, vol. 4. Buffalo, NY: Christian Literature Publishing Co., 1887. See *New Advent*, accessed Sep. 7, 2021, www.newadvent.org/fathers/14083.htm.

Dio Cassius. *Historia Romanus.* Translated by Earnest Cary. Cambridge, MA: Harvard University Press, 1914–27. See *LacusCurtius*, accessed Sep. 6, 2021, www.penelope.uchicago.edu/Thayer/E/Roman/Texts/Cassius_Dio.

Eusebius of Caesarea. *Church History.* Translated by Arthur Cushman McGiffert. In *Nicene and Post-Nicene Fathers,* Second Series, edited by Philip Schaff and Henry Wace, vol. 1, Buffalo, NY: Christian Literature Publishing Co., 1890. See *New Advent*, accessed Aug. 10, 2021, www.newadvent.org/fathers/2501.htm.

———. *The Martyrs of Palestine.* Translated by Arthur Cushman McGiffert. In *Nicene and Post-Nicene Fathers,* Second Series, edited by Philip Schaff and Henry Wace, vol. 1. Buffalo, NY: Christian Literature Publishing Co., 1890. See *New Advent*, accessed Aug. 10, 2021, www.newadvent.org/fathers/2505.htm.

Foxe, John. *Acts and Monuments.* See *Christian Classics Ethereal Library*, accessed Sep. 7, 2021, www.ccel.org/ccel/f/foxe/martyrs/files/martyrs.html.

Hippolytus. *On the Twelve Apostles.* Translated by J. H. MacMahon. In *Ante-Nicene Fathers*, edited by Alexander Roberts, James Donaldson, and A. Cleveland Coxe, vol. 5. Buffalo, NY: Christian Literature Publishing Co., 1886. See *New Advent*, accessed Aug. 10, 2021, www.newadvent.org/fathers/0524.htm.

———. *Refutation of All Heresies.* Translated by J. H. McMahon. In *Ante-Nicene Fathers*, edited by Alexander Roberts, James Donaldson, and A. Cleveland Coxe, vol. 5. Buffalo, NY: Christian Literature Publishing Co., 1886. See *New Advent*, accessed Aug. 10, 2021, www.newadvent.org/fathers/0501.htm.

Irenaeus. *Against Heresies.* Translated by Alexander Roberts and William Rambaut. In *Ante-Nicene Fathers*, edited by Alexander Roberts, James Donaldson, and A. Cleveland Coxe, vol. 1. New York: Charles Scribner's

Sons, 1903. See *New Advent*, accessed Aug. 10, 2021, www.newadvent.org/fathers/0103303.htm.

Jerome. *Lives of Illustrious Men.* Translated by Ernest Cushing Richardson. In *Nicene and Post-Nicene Fathers*, Second Series, edited by Philip Schaff and Henry Wallace, vol. 3. Buffalo, NY: Christian Literature Publishing Co., 1892. See *New Advent*, accessed Aug. 10, 2021, www.newadvent.org/fathers/2708.htm.

Justin Martyr. *Dialogue with Trypho.* Translated by Marcus Dods and George Reith. In *Ante-Nicene Fathers*, edited by Alexander Roberts, James Donaldson, and A. Cleveland Coxe, vol. 1. Buffalo, NY: Christian Literature Publishing Co., 1885. See *New Advent*, accessed Aug. 10, 2021, www.newadvent.org/fathers/0315.htm.

Origen. *On First Principles.* Translated by Frederick Crombie. In *Ante-Nicene Fathers*, edited by Alexander Roberts, James Donaldson, and A. Cleveland Coxe, vol. 4. Buffalo, NY: Christian Literature Publishing Co., 1885. See *New Advent*, accessed Aug. 10, 2021, www.newadvent.org/fathers/0412.htm.

Petrarch. *On His Own Ignorance and That of Many Others*, edited by L. M. Capelli. Paris: Honoré Champion, 1906.

Pliny the Younger. *Letters.* Translated by William Melmoth. New York: Hinds, Hoble & Eldredge, 1900. See Internet Archive, accessed Sep. 6, 2021, www.archive.org/details/lettersofplinyyo00plin.

Pontius the Deacon. *Life and Passion of St. Cyprian.* Translated by Robert Ernest Wallis. In *Ante-Nicene Fathers*, edited by Alexander Roberts, James Donaldson, and A. Cleveland Coxe, vol. 5. Buffalo, NY: Christian Literature Publishing Co., 1886. See *New Advent*, accessed Aug. 10, 2021, www.newadvent.org/fathers/0505.htm.

Severus, Sulpicius. *Sacred History.* Translated by Alexander Roberts. In *Nicene and Post-Nicene Fathers*, Second Series, edited by Philip Schaff and Henry Wace, vol. 11. Buffalo, NY: Christian Literature Publishing Co., 1894. See *New Advent*, accessed Sep. 6, 2021, www.newadvent.org/fathers/35052.htm.

Suetonius. *Lives of the Twelve Caesars.* Translated by J. C. Rolfe. Cambridge, MA: Harvard University Press, 1913–14. See *LacusCurtius*, accessed Sep. 7, 2021, www.penelope.uchicago.edu/Thayer/E/Roman/Texts/Suetonius/12Caesars/home.html.

Tacitus. *Annals.* Translated by J. Jackson. Cambridge, MA: Harvard University Press, 1925–37. See *LacusCurtius*, accessed Sep. 7, 2021, www.penelope.uchicago.edu/Thayer/E/Roman/Texts/Tacitus/home.html.

Tertullian. *On the Flesh of Christ.* Translated by Peter Holmes. In *Ante-Nicene Fathers*, edited by Alexander Roberts, James Donaldson, and A. Cleveland Coxe, vol. 3. Buffalo, NY: Christian Literature Publishing Co., 1885. See *New Advent*, accessed Aug. 10, 2021, www.newadvent.org/fathers/0315.htm.

———. *Prescription Against Heretics.* Translated by Peter Holmes. In *Ante-Nicene Fathers*, edited by Alexander Roberts, James Donaldson, and A. Cleveland

Coxe, vol. 3. Buffalo, NY: Christian Literature Publishing Co., 1885. See *New Advent*, accessed Aug. 10, 2021, www.newadvent.org/fathers/0311.htm.

## Secondary Sources

Alföldy, Géza. "The Crisis of the Third Century as Seen by Contemporaries." *Greek, Roman, and Byzantine Studies* 15, no. 1 (2003): 89–111.

Barnes, Timothy D. *Constantine: Dynasty, Religion and Power in the Later Roman Empire*. West Sussex: John Wiley and Sons, Inc., 2011.

Beard, Mary, John North, and Simon Price. *Religions of Rome: A History*. Cambridge, Eng.: Cambridge University Press, 1998.

Blumenthal, Uta-Renate, and Anne Marie Palagano. *The Investiture Controversy: Church and Monarchy from the Ninth to the Twelfth Century*. Philadelphia: University of Pennsylvania Press, 2010.

Boman, Jobjorn. "Inpulsore Cherestro? Suetonius' Divus Claudius 25.4 in Sources and Manuscripts." *Liber Annuus* 61 (2011): 355–76. www.doi.org/10.1484/J.LA.5.100355.

Brown, Raymond E. *The Death of the Messiah: From Gethsemane to the Grave*. London: Geoffrey Chapman, 1994.

Brownrigg, Ronald. *The Twelve Apostles*. New York: Macmillan, 1974.

Bushman, Richard Lyman, with Jed Woodworth. *Joseph Smith: Rough Stone Rolling*. New York: Vintage Books, 2007.

Christensen, Michael J. *C. S. Lewis on Scripture*. London: Hodder & Stoughton, 1989.

Clarke, G. W. "Some Victims of the Persecution of Maximinus Thrax." *Historia: Zeitschrift Für Alte Geschichte* 15, no. 4 (1966): 445–53. www.jstor.org/stable/4434952.

Collins, Raymond F. *1 & 2 Timothy and Titus: A Commentary*. Louisville, KY: Westminster John Knox Press, 2002.

Corcoran, Simon. "Before Constantine." In *The Cambridge Companion to the Age of Constantine*, edited by Noel Lenski. New York: Cambridge University Press, 2006, 35–58.

Corke-Webster, James. "Trouble in Pontus: The Pliny-Trajan Correspondence on the Christians Reconsidered." *TAPA* 147, no. 2 (Autumn 2017): 371–441. www.doi.org/10.1353/apa.2017.0013.

Dallmann, William. *John Hus: A Brief Story of the Life of a Martyr*. St. Louis, MO: Concordia Publishing House, 1915.

Davies, P. S. "The Origin and Purpose of the Persecution of AD 303." *The Journal of Theological Studies*, New Series, 40, no. 1 (1989): 66–94. www.jstor.org/stable/23963763.

Decret, Francois. *Early Christianity in North Africa*. London: James Clarke and Co., 2011.

Deprez, Guillaume. "Ancient Rome Thrown into the Limekiln." *Medium*, June 26, 2019, www.medium.com/@guillaume.deprez/ancient-rome-thrown-into-the-limekiln-f6b77543a5d7.

Denzey, Nicola. "What Did the Montanists Read?" *The Harvard Theological Review* 94, no. 4 (2001): 427–88. www.jstor.org/stable/3657416.

Dey, Hendrik W. *The Aurelian Wall and the Refashioning of Imperial Rome, A.D. 271–855*. Cambridge, Eng.: Cambridge University Press, 2011.

Ehrman, Bart D. "Christians Who Would Be Jews." *Lost Christianities: Christian Scriptures and the Battles of Authentication*, Audible audio ed. Chantilly, VA: The Great Courses, 2002.

————. *The New Testament: A Historical Introduction to the Early Christian Writings*. New York: Oxford University Press, 2020.

Freeman, Charles. *A.D. 381: Heretics, Pagans, and the Dawn of the Monotheistic State*. Woodstock, NY: The Overlook Press, 2009.

Frend, W. H. C. *Martyrdom and Persecution in the Early Church: A Study of Conflict from the Maccabees to Donatus*. New York: Blackwell Publishing, 1965.

Geanakoplos, Deno John. *Constantinople and the West: Essays on the Late Byzantine (Palaeologan) and Italian Renaissances and the Byzantine and Roman Churches*. Madison: University of Wisconsin Press, 1989.

Gibbon, Edward. *The History of the Decline and Fall of the Roman Empire*. New York: J. & J. Harper for Collins & Hanney, 1826.

Gilliam, J. F. "The Plague under Marcus Aurelius." *The American Journal of Philology* 82, no. 3 (1961): 225–51. www.doi.org/10.2307/292367.

Gyles, Mary Francis. "Nero Fiddled While Rome Burned." *The Classical Journal* 42, no. 4 (1947): 211–17. www.jstor.org/stable/3291751.

Hardy, Ernest George. *Christianity and the Roman Government*. London: Longmans, Green, and Co., 1894.

Harrison, P. N. *The Problem of the Pastoral Epistles*. New York: Oxford University Press, 1921.

Harper, Kyle. "People, Plagues, and Prices in the Roman World: The Evidence from Egypt." *The Journal of Economic History* 76, no. 3 (2016): 803–39. www.doi.org/10.1017/S0022050716000826.

Hengel, Martin. *Saint Peter: The Underestimated Apostle*. Grand Rapids, MI: W.B. Eerdmans Pub. Co., 2010.

Herman, Arthur. *The Cave and the Light, Plato Verses Aristotle and the Struggle for the Soul of Western Civilization*. New York: Random House, 2014.

Hopkins, Keith, and Mary Beard. *The Colosseum*. Cambridge, MA: Harvard University Press, 2011.

Hunink, Vincent. "Did Perpetua Write Her Prison Account?" *Listy Filologické / Folia Philologica* 133, no. 1/2 (2010): 147–55. www.jstor.org/stable/ 23468699.

Jackson, Kent P. *From Apostasy to Restoration.* Salt Lake City: Deseret Book Co., 1996.

———. "Leaving the Facts and the Faith." Review of *Leaving the Saints: How I Lost the Mormons and Found My Faith. FARMS Review* 17, no 1, 2005: 107–22.

Jones, F. Stanley and Patricia Duncan. "Pseudo-Clementines." *E-Clavis: Christian Apocrypha,* accessed Aug. 20, 2021, www.nasscal.com/e-clavis-christian-apocrypha/pseudo-clementines.

*Journal of Discourses.* 26 vols. Liverpool: Latter-day Saints' Book Depot, 1854–86.

Keaveney, Arthur. *Sulla Dictator.* New York: Routledge, 2005.

Keresztes, Paul. "Marcus Aurelius a Prosecutor?" *The Harvard Theological Review* 61, no. 3 (1968): 321–41. www.jstor.org/stable/1509154.

Keresztes, Paul. "Two Edicts of the Emperor Valerian." *Vigiliae Christianae* 29, no. 2 (1975): 81–95. www.doi.org/10.2307/1583165.

Kitzler, Petr. "Passio Perpetuae and Acta Perpetuae: Between Tradition and Innovation." *Listy Filologické / Folia Philologica* 130, no. 1/2 (2007): 1–19. www. jstor.org/stable/23468485.

Knipfing, John R. "The Libelli of the Decian Persecution." *The Harvard Theological Review* 16, no. 4 (1923): 345–90. www.jstor.org/stable/1507673.

Lahey, Stephen Edmund. *John Wyclif.* Great Medieval Thinkers. Oxford: Oxford University Press, 2009.

Lanzi, Fernando, and Gioia Lanzi. *Saints and Their Symbols: Recognizing Saints in Art and in Popular Images.* Collegeville, MN: Order of Saint Benedict, 2004.

Lapham, F. *An Introduction to the New Testament Apocrypha.* London: T. & T. Clark, 2004.

Lewin, Tamar. "Sikh Owner Of Gas Station Is Fatally Shot In Rampage." *New York Times,* Sep. 17, 2001.

Lightfoot, Joseph Barber, and J. R. Harmer. *Biblical Essays.* London: Macmillan & Co., 1893.

Littman, R. J., and M. L. Littman. "Galen and the Antonine Plague." *The American Journal of Philology* 94, no. 3 (1973): 243–55. www.doi.org/10.2307/ 293979.

Lyon, T. Edgar. *Apostasy to Restoration.* Salt Lake City: Deseret Book Co., 1960.

MacCulloch, Diarmaid. *Christianity: The First Three Thousand Years.* New York: Penguin Books, 2011.

MacDonald, Dennis R. *Does the New Testament Imitate Homer?: Four Cases from the Acts of the Apostles.* New Haven, CT: Yale University, 2003.

McBirnie, William Steuart. *The Search for the Twelve Apostles*. Wheaton, IL: Tyndale House Publishers, 1973.

McBrien, Richard P. *Lives of the Popes: The Pontiffs from St. Peter to Benedict XVI*. San Francisco: Harper, 2006.

McConkie, Bruce R. *Mormon Doctrine*. Salt Lake City: Bookcraft, 1958.

———. "Our Relationship with the Lord," BYU Speeches, Mar. 1982, www. speeches.byu.edu/talks/bruce-r-mcconkie/relationship-lord/.

Meier, John P. "The Circle of the Twelve: Did It Exist during Jesus' Public Ministry?" *Journal of Biblical Literature* 116, no. 4 (1997): 635–72. www.doi. org/10.2307/3266551.

———. *A Marginal Jew: Rethinking the Historical Jesus*. New Haven, CT: Yale University Press, 2016.

Metzger, Bruce M. *The Canon of the New Testament: Its Origin, Development, and Significance*. Oxford: Clarendon Press, 1987.

Millar, Fergus. *The Emperor in the Roman World*. New York: Cornell University Press, 1977.

Mommsen, Theodor. "Petrarch's Conception of the 'Dark Ages.'" *Speculum* 17, no. 2 (Apr. 1942): 226–42. www.jstor.org/stable/2856364.

Mosheim, Johann Lorenz. *Institutes of Ecclesiastical History*. Translated by James Murdock. London: William Tegg, 1968.

Moss, Candida R. *The Myth of Persecution: How Early Christians Invented a Story of Martyrdom*. New York: Harper One, 2014.

Musurillo, Herbert. *The Acts of the Christian Martyrs. Introduction, Texts and Translations*. Oxford: Clarendon Press, 1972.

Niebuhr, Barthold Georg. *Lectures on the History of Rome, from the Earliest Times to the Fall of the Western Empire*. London: C. Taylor, 1898.

Nibley, Hugh. *The Passing of the Church: Forty Variations on an Unpopular Theme*. Provo, UT: Foundation for Ancient Research & Mormon Studies, 1975.

O'Loughlin, Thomas. *The Didache: A Window on the Earliest Christians*. Grand Rapids, MI: Baker Academic, 2010.

Pagels, Elaine. *Beyond Belief: The Secret Gospel of Thomas*. New York: Random House, 2003.

Perkins, Judith. *The Suffering Self: Pain and Narrative Representation in the Early Christian Era*. London: Routledge, 2007.

Perrin, Norman, Dennis C. Duling, and Robert L. Ferm. *The New Testament: An Introduction: Proclamation and Parenesis, Myth and History*. San Diego: Harcourt Brace College Publishers, 1994.

Plinius and Betty Radice. *The Letters of the Younger Pliny*. Harmondsworth, Middlesex: Penguin Books, 1969.

Polhill, John B. *Acts*. Nashville: Broadman Press, 2001.

Potter, D. S. *Prophecy and History in the Crisis of the Roman Empire: A Historical Commentary on the Thirteenth Sibylline Oracle*. Oxford: Clarendon Press, 2011.

———. *The Roman Empire at Bay: AD 180–395*. London: Routledge, 2009.

Quasten, Johannes. *Patrology: The Beginnings of Patristic Literature*. Utrecht-Antwerp: Spectrum Publishers, 1962.

Reiner, Rob, dir. *The Princess Bride*. 1987; Los Angeles: Twentieth Century Fox, 2014. DVD.

Reynolds, Noel B. *Early Christians in Disarray: Contemporary LDS Perspectives on the Christian Apostasy*. Provo, UT: Foundation for Ancient Research and Mormon Studies, 2005.

Rhodes, James Montague. "Acts of Andrew and Matthias." In *The New Testament*. Oxford: Clarendon Press, 1924.

Riley, Gregory J. *Resurrection Reconsidered: Thomas and John in Controversy*. Minneapolis: Fortress Press, 1995.

Rives, James B. "The Persecution of Christians and Ideas of Community in the Roman Empire." In *Politiche Religiose nel Mondo Antico e Tardoantico*, edited by G. A. Cecconi and C. Gabrielli. Bari: Edipuglia, 2011. www.academia.edu/5382548.

Rives, James B. "The Decree of Decius and the Religion of Empire." *The Journal of Roman Studies* 89 (1999): 135–54. www.doi.org/10.2307/300738.

Roberts, B. H. *Outlines of Ecclesiastical History*. Salt Lake City: Deseret News, 1902.

Robinson, Jonathan William. *William of Ockham's Early Theory of Property Rights in Context*. Leiden: Brill, 2012.

Robinson, O. F. *The Criminal Law of Ancient Rome*. London: Gerald Duckworth & Co. Ltd., 1995.

Rougé, Jean. "L'incendie de Rome en 64 et l'incendie de Nicomédie en 303." *In Mélanges d'histoire Ancienne Offerts* à William Seston, edited by William Seston. Paris: Boccard, 1974.

Sage, Michael M. "The Persecution of Valerian and the Peace of Gallienus." *Wiener Studien* 96 (1963): 137–59. www.jstor.org/stable/24746544.

Scofield, C. I., and E. Schuyler English. *The New Scofield Reference Bible: Holy Bible, Authorized King James Version, with Introductions, Annotations, Subject Chain References, and Such Word Changes in the Text as Will Help the Reader*. New York: Oxford University Press, 1982.

Sharp, Mary. *A Traveller's Guide to the Churches of Rome*. London: Evelyn, 1967.

Shaw, Brent D. "The Passion of Perpetua." *Past & Present* 139 (1993): 3–45. www.jstor.org/stable/651089.

Shelton, W. Brian. *Quest for the Historical Apostles: Tracing Their Lives and Legacies*. Grand Rapids, MI: Baker Academic, 2018.

Smith, Carl B. *No Longer Jews: The Search for Gnostic Origins*. Peabody, MA: Hendrickson Publishers, 2004.

Smith, Joseph Fielding. *Answers to Gospel Questions*. Salt Lake City: Deseret Book Co., 1957.

Smith, Joseph Jr. et al. *History of the Church of Jesus Christ of Latter-day Saints*, edited by B. H. Roberts. 7 vols. Salt Lake City: Deseret News Press, 1902–12, 1932.

Southern, Pat. *The Roman Empire from Severus to Constantine*. London: Routledge, 2015.

Špiclová, Zdeňka and Kaše, Vojtěch. "Distant Reading of the Gospel of Thomas and the Gospel of John: Reflection of Methodological Aspects of the Use of Digital Technologies in the Research of Biblical Texts." *Open Theology* 6, no. 1 (2020): 423-39. www.doi.org/10.1515/opth-2020-0111

Stark, Rodney. *Cities of God: The Real Story of How Christianity Became an Urban Movement and Conquered Rome*. New York: HarperOne, 2007.

Syme, Ronald. *The Roman Revolution*. Oxford: Oxford University Press, 1960.

Talmage, James E. *The Great Apostasy*. Salt Lake City: The Deseret News, 1909.

Thomas, Gabor, et al. "Technology, Ritual and Anglo-Saxon Agriculture: The Biography of a Plough Coulter from Lyminge, Kent." *Antiquity* 90, no. 351 (June 2016): 742–58. www.dx.doi.org/10.15184/aqy.2016.73.

Thompson, James Westfall. "The Alleged Persecution of the Christians at Lyons in 177." *The American Journal of Theology* 16, no. 3 (July 1912): 359–84. www.jstor.org/stable/3154941.

Thompson, Leonard L. "The Martyrdom of Polycarp: Death in the Roman Games." *The Journal of Religion* 82, no. 1 (2002): 27–52. jstor.org/stable/1205882.

Vogel, Dan, ed. *History of Joseph Smith and the Church of Jesus Christ of Latter-day Saints: A Source- and Text-Critical Edition*. 8 vols. Salt Lake City: Smith-Pettit Foundation, 2015.

Welch, John W. "Modern Revelation: A Guide to Research about the Apostasy." In *Early Christians in Disarray*, edited by Noel B. Ryenolds. Provo, UT: Brigham Young University Press, 1995.

Wenham, John. "Did Peter Go to Rome in AD 42?" *Tyndale Bulletin* 23 (1972).

# INDEX